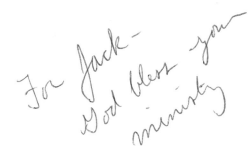

Taking the Plunge

BAPTISM
and PARENTING

Anne E. Kitch

MOREHOUSE PUBLISHING
an imprint of
Church Publishing Incorporated
Harrisburg • New York

Morehouse Publishing, P.O. Box 1321, Harrisburg, PA 17105

Morehouse Publishing, 445 Fifth Avenue, New York, NY 10016

Morehouse Publishing is an imprint of Church Publishing Incorporated.

Cover art: Detail of water splash, courtesy of Jupiter Images

Cover design: Lee Singer

Library of Congress Cataloging-in-Publication Data

Kitch, Anne E.
  Taking the plunge : baptism and parenting / Anne E. Kitch.
    p. cm.
  Includes bibliographical references.
  ISBN-13: 978-0-8192-2185-8 (pbk.)
  1. Infant baptism. 2. Parenting—Religious aspects—Christianity. 3. Child rearing—Religious aspects—Christianity. I. Title.
BV813.3.K58 2006
248.8'45—dc22
                              2006031468

Printed in the United States of America

06 07 08 09   10 9 8 7 6 5 4 3 2 1

For Jim Peck

CONTENTS

ACKNOWLEDGMENTS

Just as we cannot live a baptized life in isolation, a book like this cannot be written apart from community. First and foremost, I want to thank Debra Farrington, my good friend and former publisher, for being there to hear the first inkling of this book and to ensure that it would find its way to completion. And I continue to be grateful to my editor, Nancy Fitzgerald, for her kind and astute guidance, and to Ryan Masteller and all of the wonderful folks at Morehouse for their truly caring way of working.

I am grateful to all who helped along the way by reading (and rereading) portions of this work, including Sharon Albert, Peter D'Angio, and my writing sisters. I am especially grateful to my friend and mentor Thomas Breidenthal for carefully checking my theology and to Betsy Roadman for helping craft excellent discussion questions; any failings in these areas are mine alone. This work would be lifeless without all of the parenting stories my friends were willing to share; my thanks to Linda Betjeman, Addie Clark, Rick Cluett, Eric Hinds, J. Carr Holland, Karen Kitabwalla, Canon Bill Lewellis, Dorothy Linthicum, Catherine S. Roskam, Wendy Urban-Meade, and Beth Vorosmarti, fabulous and faithful parents all! I also want to thank all of the people I have prepared for baptism; my own understanding of baptism has been influenced by their questions, thoughtful comments, and love of their children.

Finally, I thank my husband, Jim, and our daughters, Sophie and Lucy, who make our home one full of love and silliness and dancing and faith. This is their story as much as mine, and they were very gracious in sharing it. I offer this work in loving memory of Douglas Brown, OHC, my spiritual guide and Sophie's godfather, who told me I should write this book the same day that I came to tell him I was thinking of writing it. May his soul and the souls of all the departed through the mercy of God rest in peace.

INTRODUCTION

*Come, Holy Spirit, fill the hearts of your people
and enkindle in them the fire of your love.*

—Traditional prayer

I used to think I knew everything about preparing parents for the baptism
of their child. Then I became a parent and had my own baptism by fire.
Before parenthood, I spent a lot of time as a parish priest designing and
implementing pre-baptismal instruction programs for parents who wanted
their children to be baptized. I prepared adults for baptism as well, but that
is a topic for another book. Baptismal preparation looks fairly similar in
most Episcopal parishes. Generally parents fill out an application provided
by the parish, meet with one of the clergy to talk about the meaning of baptism, and finally attend one or more classes during which the history, theology, and implications of baptism are discussed. The parish I worked at as a
newly ordained priest followed this basic pattern. As baptism is the ritual
that not only signifies but also brings about entrance into the Christian faith
and life, the clergy at that parish wanted to equip parents for the task of raising children in the Christian faith. We asked that the parents choose godparents in consultation with their priest. We required parents and godparents to
attend three classes prior to the baptism. If the godparents lived out of town
and were not able to attend, we asked the parents to choose an additional,
local godparent—perhaps a member of the parish—who could. Finally,

there was a rehearsal the day before the baptism at which more instruction took place.

At the time, each of these elements seemed vitally important to me. I wanted parents to understand that baptism was much more than a nice service to honor the birth of their child. I wanted them to know it was more than obtaining God's blessing for their baby. I wanted them to know it was more than one day in church. I wanted them to understand that baptism is a life-long commitment to the church and to a life of faith. We had many baptisms in that parish, and for a couple of years, I forged ahead, enthusiastic about the teaching and stringent about the requirements.

Then I became pregnant with my own child. I have to tell you, things looked a lot different from that perspective. For one thing, I discovered how difficult it is to choose godparents. My husband and I had long discussions about it. Who would we want to be involved with our yet-to-be-born child? His family had a tradition of choosing relatives as godparents. Mine did not. I knew who my godparents were but was no longer close to them. We wanted people who would be involved with our child for life. We wanted people we enjoyed, people who knew us well and were serious about their faith. It was harder than I could have imagined.

But we finally agreed on two friends and invited them to be the godparents of our yet-to-be-born first child. We even selected the baptismal date before the baby had arrived. I was due in late September, so we chose All Saints' Sunday, the first Sunday in November and a traditional baptismal day in the church calendar. I thought we were all set.

But our daughter Sophia waited until the first week of October to put in her appearance, so she was only a month old at her baptism. In the weeks leading up to it, I dutifully attended the baptism classes that the parish offered. But these looked a lot different too, when seen through the lens of postpartum sleep deprivation. For one thing, my husband's work schedule made it impossible for him to attend. For another, I found out how difficult it was to get an infant fed each day, much less dressed and out of the house to attend an evening event on time. Most evenings I was exhausted and in no condition to learn something new. The godparents we'd carefully selected didn't live in town and couldn't attend the classes, and we didn't want to choose an additional one. So I excused us from that particular requirement.

After all, one of her godparents was a parish priest and one was a monk. I didn't think they needed baptismal instruction. Nor did I want to choose someone else I didn't know as well to be that close to my child.

The day before the baptism, relatives began to arrive in town and I was still struggling to find something festive to wear that fit my postpartum body. That night I dreamed that my mother-in-law, deceased for several years, arrived at our door to be with her first grandchild at this important event. The next day we dressed Sophie in the family baptismal gown that had been worn by three generations of children; then we all went to church. I have pictures to prove it—a good thing, because I was so exhausted that I hardly remember the event, and I certainly didn't have the energy to enjoy it fully.

After that, I changed a lot about the way I helped families prepare for baptism. For one thing, I recommended that parents wait until their child was more than a month old—the service and celebration are a lot more fun if you're awake for them. For another, I required fewer classes and became much more flexible about who should attend them.

I still believe that baptism is a significant event in the life of a family and the life of a parish. And I believe that preparation for it is vital. But now I understand that parents and children have a lifetime to learn about the significance of baptism—and I know it's impossible to learn it all up front. Baptism is more than one powerful moment during a church service. It's about raising a child in the faith. It puts a frame around everything that happens for the rest of the baby's life.

Crossing the Threshold

Baptism is a threshold experience. It's about moving through a doorway from one room to another, from one space to another, from one community to another. The baptismal service is the moment you stand on the threshold. But you don't stay there. Before baptism, people belong to the community of their family and are beloved of God. After baptism, they still belong to the community of their family—and God still loves them. But now they also belong to a larger community—a vast extended family known as the Church. Just like the rooms on each side of a doorway, both communities exist before and after the baptism. Yet after the baptism, both communities are changed. The church community gains a member. The family community, including the newly baptized, is embraced by a larger community within which they are invited to live a life of faith. After all, the Church is the gathered community of all the baptized. Those who have been baptized now know both communities. They've gained a wider understanding of the people of God. And with the arrival of new members, the people of God know a little more about who they are.

Baptism is a Holy Spirit moment. I often warn people that they don't want to mess with the Holy Spirit unless they're willing to face the consequences. We don't invite the Holy Spirit into our lives and remain unchanged—and that change doesn't end at the baptismal font. What happens in baptism is much more than the rite itself. Ultimately it's about where it leads you, how it changes the communities to which you belong, and how it changes you. All of the relationships shift. Thus, it's important to prepare for this transition. It's important for parents to prepare themselves as they bring their child to the baptismal waters. It's important for the community to prepare to welcome a new member of the body of Christ. And it's vitally important for the individual, the family, and the community to continue to develop a full and rich faith life. Baptism doesn't gift us with a mature faith—it ushers us into a community actively striving toward a mature life of faith. With baptism comes a commitment to this life of faith; this commitment involves a growth process. Just as we develop physically, socially, and psychologically, we also grow spiritually. With each new baptism, not only does the newly baptized embark on this life of faith, but the members of the Christian community recommit themselves to this journey as well. They promise once again to grow in their understanding of God's will for them, to develop a moral stance based on the teachings of Christ, and to become more loving people. Life for the baptized is not lived in isolation but is intentionally placed in the context of the Christian community.

This is why baptisms occur on a Sunday morning during the Eucharist, within the gathered community of the people of God. In one sense, the baptism is about the individual who is being baptized. After all, in the church we baptize people one by one and by name. Yet each individual is baptized into the Church—the community of faith that we also call the body of Christ. Through baptism, an individual is welcomed into the community of faith.

So not just the individual is changed, but the entire community is changed as well. Baptism isn't something we should do lightly; it requires forethought, preparation, and the understanding that this is just the beginning.

Being Part of the Community

Bringing your child to the baptismal font but not participating in the life of the Christian community would be a bit like signing your child up for Little League but never bringing her to the ball field. You'd hardly consider your child an active member of the team if she never attended a practice or played in a game. This would be a loss not only for your child, but for the team as well. Your child wouldn't learn what the team had to offer in regard to pitching, batting, catching, and working as a team—or enjoy the fun and friendship of teammates. The team would miss out as well. The other kids wouldn't gain from the gifts your child had to offer, from athletic abilities to people skills. A great deal of being part of a team means showing up.

The same is true about being faithful to the Christian community. When you participate in the community, you gain many of the same things you would gain from playing on a ball team. You learn skills and strategies to help you become a stronger player. You get to know your teammates, some of whom become friends. You have fun. The community benefits from all that you have to offer as well. Your gifts are identified and developed and added to the collected wisdom of the team. Your offering of yourself brings joy to the community.

Parents who bring their children to be baptized are sometimes active members of the parish and sometimes not. Regardless of their level of involvement, most parents say the same things when I ask them why they want their child to be baptized. They want something good for their child. They want their child to be blessed by God. They want their child to believe in God. They went to Sunday school when they were children, and they think it's a good idea to bring their child to Sunday school too. But the thing is, the baptism ritual is only the doorway. Participation in the life of the Church is what brings individuals all the joy and love and support that a Christian life has to offer. It's what happens after the baptism—how the baptism is lived into—that makes a lifelong difference. Baptism is signing your child up for a life in Christ. You still need to get them to the practices and games so they'll learn and grow and love as Christians.

The Power of Ritual

Picture a graduation ceremony—any graduation ceremony. You can't miss the symbols that mark it—from the funny hats that fit no one's head, to the gowns that some participants always forget to iron, to the rolled-up parchment diplomas. Graduation even has its own sort of secular liturgy, with readings and songs and speeches that sound a lot like sermons. As human beings, we are drawn to ritual. Rituals—actions that are coordinated, repeated, and meaningful—are powerful, and religious rituals are particularly potent.[1] Many rituals use strong symbols. Through rituals, we enact who we are. They provide identity, connection, and stability.

Like any ritual, Christian baptism has a particular shape and a set of symbols. When I ask a group of parents and godparents what comes to mind when they think of baptism, they quickly come up with the symbols: a church, water, the font, babies dressed in white. Rituals are easily recognized in our society. They have power because of what they do. They provide a sense of identity and stability. They make us comfortable. The baptism ritual connects us to the community of the church. Giving birth to or adopting a child is a big deal. Participating in a ritual marks this rite of passage. We have become parents, and we want the world to recognize our new role. We want to do something loving for our child. And what could give more recognition and be more loving than a big fancy ceremony in a church? I believe that parents who have no particular interest in the lifelong nurture of Christian faith may still have a great interest in baptizing their child. Baptism is the ritual available to them to celebrate this birth or adoption.

Fear of the Unknown

When my daughter Sophie was born, the hospital staff seemed somewhat amazed at the number of clerics who were suddenly seen in the maternity ward. Among them was my bishop, who came and prayed the "Thanksgiving for the Birth or Adoption of a Child" with us (BCP 439).[2] She ministered to us in a moment that was both joyful and fearful. The labor and birth had been difficult, and she talked with us about the way that birth could be a terrifying experience—being a mother herself, she would know.

The bishop also talked about the biblical tradition of purification after childbirth. When their children were several weeks old, Jewish women would come to the temple for a rite of purification. The Gospel of Luke (2:22) records how Mary, the mother of Jesus, performed this ritual. It was similar to the one the Jewish priests used to purify themselves before entering the presence of the ark of the covenant, considered a dangerous place to be. Tradition told them that no one could see God face to face and live, so to be in the presence of the ark and commune with Yahweh was to stand at a point between life and death. It was terrifying and holy.

Childbirth may be seen in the same way. To give birth is to stand between life and death. It is terrifying and holy. The dangers are very real. Yet it is also to be in the presence of God. So in the Jewish tradition the purification ritual after birth acknowledged the powerful experience that that woman had undergone in giving birth. It recognized that she had stood on the threshold of death and just about looked God in the face.[3]

Parents often bring their children to be baptized out of fear, thinking of baptism as protection. If their children are baptized, they reason, they'll be safe from ultimate death. A baptized child may die in this world but still gain access to eternal life and the kingdom of heaven. Some parents fear that a child who dies before baptism won't go to heaven. While there is no support for such a belief in current Anglican teaching, this fear motivates people. I don't think if push came to shove that most parents, even those basically unchurched, would believe that a loving God would abandon an innocent child. But the power of baptism as a ritual of belonging—to a community and to God—causes people to seek it out whether they really understand it or not.

Baptism Changes Parents

Baptism is a threshold experience for parents as well. Sometimes parents are very aware of this reality. They find their own faith awakened as they contemplate wanting the best for their child. Other parents remain oblivious to the power present when the Holy Spirit is invoked at baptism. Yet while these parents may not understand much of what happens in the ritual of baptism, they know they want it.

Childbirth in the twenty-first century is less terrifying than it was in first-century Palestine, but that primal fear still remains. In the act of pouring water over the baby's head—and gathering in the embrace of a loving community—there is comfort and support for the new parents. The baptism ritual in the church is also a moment of change for parents, particularly first-time parents. Outwardly, all that happens to babies is that some water is poured over their heads, to which they may or may not react. But inwardly, spiritually, much more is at stake, and what happens to the parents and godparents—those responsible for the child—is profound. The ritual shows explicitly that they are not alone in the business of parenting. It has been done before. Many other parents have brought their children to the baptismal waters and survived. They have survived baptism and parenting, and their children have lived to tell the tale. The baptismal service implicitly tells them that God is present in their life together and that God will provide. The baptismal rite itself offers guideposts to help parents deal with all that comes next. It creates a path of light to follow in the darkness that lies ahead in the unknown territory of raising a child.

While the fear that God will reject their child or somehow punish the unbaptized is not based on truth, there is a much more real and valid fear that all parents face and one that baptism does speak to. People are scared of being parents. Scared of how the world might hurt their child. Scared of how *they* might hurt their child. Scared of how their child might hurt them. Scared of all the hurts they won't be able to protect themselves or their child from. Baptism in some sense mitigates this fear. Yes, parenting will be difficult and dangerous and sometimes even terrifying. But by having your child baptized, you are choosing not to be in it alone. You and your child will emerge from the baptismal waters empowered with the gifts of the Hoy Spirit and the witness of a church community that has done this before.

The Meaning of Baptism

Baptism changes everything. It propelled Jesus from life in the village to the most powerful ministry in human history. It empowered the apostles to become courageous preachers of the Word. And it transforms people today into members of the body of Christ. A little water and a few words can do all this. But what really happens when the priest pours water over a baby's head? What really happens in baptism? In the Christian tradition, we believe that through baptism, God adopts us as children. We become members of the Church, the body of Christ. We receive forgiveness of sins. We're given new life through the gift of the Holy Spirit.

But baptism didn't begin with the Christian church. Jesus himself, a devout Jew, was baptized by John in the Jordan River. The story of Jesus' baptism is told in all four Gospels—Matthew, Mark, Luke, and John. Scripture tells us that John the Baptist was a great preacher who called the Jewish people to repent of their sins and seek God's forgiveness. People were baptized—the word "baptize" comes from a Greek word meaning "to immerse"—by John in the Jordan River as they confessed their sins. John's was a baptism of repentance. As he preached, he talked of one who would come after him who would be greater, telling the people, "I have baptized you with water; but he will baptize you with the Holy Spirit" (Mark 1:8; see also Matthew 3:11 and Luke 3:16).

Then Jesus came on the scene and asked John to baptize *him*. John was a bit flummoxed by the request. After all, he wasn't worthy to baptize the Son of God. And surely God's Son, the messiah, didn't need forgiveness of sins— but John baptized him anyway. As Jesus came out of the water, something different happened. The Holy Spirit descended on him in the shape of a dove, and a voice from heaven said, "This is my Son, my beloved." So with Jesus, baptism wasn't merely about repentance and forgiveness; it was also about welcoming the Holy Spirit.

Jesus was an adult when he was baptized, so his baptism had little to do with his parents raising him in the faith. They committed to do that when they presented him in the temple as an infant. But the way Jesus lived his life did change after baptism. It was after his baptism that he began his public ministry. Immediately after his baptism, he was driven into the wilderness, where he was tempted and tested and forced to claim his true identity. Then he returned to civilization, where he began to teach and heal and gather disciples. For about three years, he was fully engaged in the ministry of proclaiming God's love to the people. Then he was crucified. But as it turned out, killing the Son of God didn't end God's love. Jesus was raised from the dead, and his teaching continued to spread.

After his resurrection, Jesus met his disciples and instructed them to carry on his work, sending them forth with these words: "Go therefore and make disciples of all nations, baptizing them in the name of the Father and of the Son and of the Holy Spirit, and teaching them to obey everything that I have commanded you" (Matthew 28:19). We use these same words today when we baptize: "Claire, I baptize you in the name of the Father and of the Son and of the Holy Spirit." So the baptism that we understand in the Christian church of the twenty-first century is one that began with Jesus and his followers.

Baptism in the Early Church

As baptismal rites developed in the early church, they included water and the words "in the name of the Father and of the Son and of the Holy Spirit." Baptism was normally administered by a bishop.[4] As the church grew and changed, baptismal preparation and church rituals became more complex. The Great Vigil of Easter and the Feast of Pentecost became traditional days for baptisms. Candidates were prepared through instruction, which often took months or even years, and were then examined before the baptism. What we know as the Apostles' Creed was an early baptismal examination. Candidates for baptism were asked, "Do you believe in God the Father?" They answered, "I believe in God the Father almighty, maker of heaven and earth." Next they were asked, "Do you believe in Jesus Christ?" and finally, "Do you believe in the Holy Spirit?" As they answered each question correctly, they were immersed in or sprinkled with water. Once baptized, they immediately took their place in the life and worship of the Christian community.

In the early years, most of those baptized were adult converts. There is evidence that entire households, probably including the children, were baptized at the same time. The tradition of infant baptism developed over the years. It was understood that infants couldn't be prepared for baptism or speak the baptismal promises for themselves; thus, the tradition of parents and godparents as sponsors developed. These adults spoke on behalf of the candidates who were too young to speak for themselves. For these parents, presenting a child for baptism was pledging to teach that child the faith so the child would grow up being formed by the Christian community. It was never assumed that one must understand all of the teachings of Jesus and every aspect of the faith of the church in order to be baptized. But it was assumed that the only reason to be baptized was to take one's place in the life of the church.

Baptism Today

Today we continue the rite of baptism. In the Anglican tradition, both children and adults may come to be baptized. The two elements necessary for baptism are water and the use of the words "in the name of the Father and of the Son and of the Holy Spirit." Holy Baptism is considered a complete initiation into the Christian faith. In other words, once you're baptized, you're in! Through baptism, an unbreakable bond is established between God and an individual. Candidates presented for baptism are examined or questioned about their acceptance of the Christian faith. They make vows to follow the teachings of Jesus. For infants or children too young to speak for themselves, parents and godparents make the promises for them. These sponsors present their children for baptism and then are examined on behalf of the children. Then the gathered community is asked to support these new members of the body of Christ. The entire assembly joins in saying the Baptismal Covenant, an expanded form of the ancient Apostles' Creed. The bishop or priest then prays over the water, and each candidate is baptized by name. The gathered community welcomes those who are newly baptized, who have the rest of their lives to figure it all out.

Why Read This Book?

This book is for parents and godparents who have presented a child for baptism and are asking, "Now what? I've just made all these promises—how do I keep them? How do I raise a child in the Christian faith? What does it mean to raise a child to the full stature of Christ?" This book explores just that. What is baptism, what promises are made in baptism, and just how are you going to fulfill them? My hope is to explain what the promises mean and then provide guidance in how to live them out. Baptism is about the start of a life of faith in the Christian church. How you live it out is entirely up to you.

Part 1 of this book takes us through the baptismal service from The Book of Common Prayer. Chapter 1 begins with the presentation of the child. Just what does it mean to present someone for baptism? Chapters 2 and 3 look at the examination of the candidates. What promises do parents make, and what do they mean? What does this mean for everyday life? Chapter 4 deals with the importance of the gathered community. What does it mean to be a member of the body of Christ? What does the church community have to do with your child? Chapter 5 explores the Baptismal Covenant as a guideline for a Christian life, and chapter 6 examines the baptism itself.

Part 2 of this book crosses the threshold of the baptismal service in the church and enters the home. Now that the party is over and the family christening gown is packed away once again, what can you do to nurture your faith and the faith of your child day by day in your home? Chapters 7 through 11 explore family rituals, prayer, respect for family members, the importance of manners, and much more. If you're looking for practical wisdom, you may want to jump ahead to these chapters.

At the end of each chapter is a section titled "Getting Your Feet Wet." These sections offer questions for individual contemplation or group discussion along with parenting tips and ideas to try at home. The concept behind this book is not so much "how to" as "why not?" Why not make faith formation part of daily parenting? Why not see raising children as an opportunity to deepen your own faith life? Why not live into your baptism? I hope the myriad stories told in these pages will delight you and shed light upon your parenting path.

PART 1
The Baptismal Service

I get very excited conducting baptismal services. First there is the anticipation of the event. Since I have usually prepared all the candidates and their sponsors, I know who is going to be there and have a personal connection with them. I know the boy who spent the first six weeks of his life in intensive care, the mother who is being baptized along with her three-month-old twins, and the family who just moved into town and is hoping that this congregation will be their spiritual home. I think about them and pray for them, the week before, the night before. There is anxiety as well. I can't seem to get through the hours leading up to the service without picking up some of the apprehension of the parents and families. Will everyone be there on time? Will I remember the babies' names? Did I remind the ushers to rope off the pews for the candidates? Are the parents happy about the event?

If I have time, I check the church before the service begins to see if everything is in place. But on some busy Sundays I am moving so rapidly from one thing to the next, from leading an adult forum to checking on the acolytes to praying with the choir to getting myself ready, that I have to trust that the altar guild and everyone else has it all in place. I scan the pews at the last minute to see if everyone is there.

Suddenly it all begins and ready or not, here we go. The acolytes and choir line up, the baptismal candidates and their families are in place and we begin to sing the opening hymn of the service. I can sense a certain bounce in my step. My joy at the event increases as the service takes a sharp turn immediately after the sermon and heads straight into the presentation of the candidates. A dialogue begins, first between me (as the celebrant) and the sponsors presenting those to be baptized. But soon the entire congregation is on its feet as we recite the Baptismal Covenant in question and answer form. I feel the congregation's enthusiasm too, as they not only witness the candidates about to be baptized, but recommit themselves to a life of faith as well. I am practically singing at this point as I call out the baptismal questions and a church packed with people responds in full voice.

"Do you believe in God . . . ?" the questions begin.

"I believe . . ." some 300 voices answer back.

"Will you . . . ?"

"I will, with God's help."

The questions are both familiar and new to me each time.

Then we march to the font, candidates and sponsors and parents. The children of the congregation crowd around so that they can see. As I gather each child into my arms, my anxiety about remembering their names is replaced by sheer delight. I scoop up handfuls of water dousing their foreheads as I baptize in God's name. Following their dousing at the font, the newly baptized gather at the front of the congregation and are enthusiastically welcomed. Later, as I see the new Christians and their families at the communion rail, I rejoice as all are fed.

At one memorable service, I baptized seven people: one adult, a nine-year-old, a five-year-old, and four infants. As I completed the rite for the last child I looked up and asked the congregation, "Anyone else?" It seemed like we had baptized the entire world that morning and we all felt the momentum of the Holy Spirit pushing us on.

While the rite remains the same for each baptismal service I lead, I know that each candidate follows a different path to the baptismal waters. Some are more prepared than others. All become part of something larger than themselves: the community known as the Church. None enter that community empty-handed. They bring themselves and their gifts.

The apostle Paul knew this about God's people: that we all come to the baptismal waters bearing different gifts and that no one emerges from those waters unchanged. Baptism is the calling of all Christians. And, as with any calling, it carries responsibilities. Imprisoned for his beliefs, Paul wrote to the Christian community at Ephesus:

> *I therefore, the prisoner in the Lord, beg you to lead a life worthy of the calling to which you have been called, with all humility and gentleness, with patience, bearing with one another in love, making every effort to maintain the unity of the Spirit in the bond of peace. There is one body and one Spirit, just as you were called to the one hope of your calling, one Lord, one faith, one baptism, one God and Father of all, who is above all and through all and in all. (Ephesians 4:1–6)*

We are reminded of this call as the baptismal service in the Book of Common Prayer begins with this dialogue:

Celebrant	There is one Body and one Spirit
People	There is one hope in God's call to us
Celebrant	One Lord, one Faith, one Baptism
People	One God and Father of all.

The shape and the content of the baptism service is joyful and demanding as it ushers us into a life in which values such as humility, gentleness, patience, and love are paramount.

There are many Christian denominations and many baptismal services. What follows in part 1 of this book is an examination of the baptismal service in the Book of Common Prayer of the Episcopal Church. It has its own form and questions. But the theology behind it would be familiar to many denominations and the stories recognizable to any parent. Whether you are a parent contemplating for the first time the baptism of your child, or a veteran of many such services, there is much food for thought in the chapters that follow. May they engage you in your own dialogue with the baptismal service and the Holy Spirit.

CHAPTER ONE

Introducing . . . !

When my second daughter, Lucy, was baptized, we had been in our new parish for about six months. I remember the flurry of activity surrounding the event: preparing for the arrival of family and godparents from out of town, coordinating meals and celebrations, and, once again, finding something festive to wear that fit my postpartum body. I was back to work in the parish after maternity leave, but my choice was to be in the pew as mother rather than at the font as priest that day. Even so, my clergy eye checked the readiness of the church.

The pews at the front of the church had been roped off for the candidates and their families. Our daughter would share her baptismal day with another daughter of the parish. As we took our place in the front row, a few of the regulars were displaced from their usual pews, a shuffle that always happens on baptismal days. The font was ready. The cover of the font, with its Holy Spirit dove counterweight, had been lifted to reveal the large stone basin with water in the bottom. More water was at hand in a large silver pitcher ready to be poured into the font in an abundant stream that would be visible to the congregation. A shell with the oil of chrism, blessed by the bishop the previous holy week, stood ready along with two new baptismal candles. There were also two small wrapped packages that I knew had been prepared by the first-grade Sunday school class. A student from that class would present one of the gifts to us—a Bible-story book about the baptism of Jesus by John.

The acolytes, choir, and clergy lined up at the back of the church, and as the music for the opening hymn began, so did the procession. My daughter rested contentedly in my lap. I had nursed her, changed her diaper, and dressed her in the same baptismal gown that her sister had worn—the one that had now clothed four generations of new Christians in my family. I hoped she would remain content, at least until the baptismal moment itself.

There were the opening prayers, the lessons, and the sermon to get through before the actual baptism. It's always a risky thing to place too much hope in an infant's contentment. As the procession passed our pew, she began to squirm, and I tried to settle her again. The squirming increased, and I began to wonder if the choir members would notice my struggle. What would they think of their new priest, who couldn't keep her child calm during a service? What if my daughter began to scream and I had to get up and leave the pew before the baptism?

I don't remember what the scripture readings were that day, but I do remember that the sermon had something to do with baptism. Miraculously, my daughter never did break into full cry, and suddenly the moment had arrived. "The candidates for holy baptism will now be present-ed," said the celebrant. And there we were—me and my husband and the three godparents—standing up and saying, "I present Lucy Grace to receive the sacrament of baptism."

The Presentation

Parents and godparents, the sponsors, often stumble over this line: "I present Calvin to receive the sacrament of baptism." When I prepare people for a bap-tism, I always have them rehearse it out loud. Speaking this line during the baptismal liturgy can be more difficult than people think. Often this is because the parents and godparents aren't used to speaking up in church. Often it's because the moment to speak seems to come upon them suddenly and they're caught unawares even though they rehearsed the day before. But I think there is another reason people tend to trip over this line or mumble it: they're hesitant about the power of the words they are about to invoke. Presenting a child to a church community and to God is no small thing.

What exactly does it mean to present someone for baptism? What does it mean to say those words in church, in the midst of the gathered communi-ty, and before God? In everyday terms, to present means to bring into the presence of someone or to introduce. It also means to make a gift to some-one, to give. When you present your child for baptism, you are doing all of these things. First, you're introducing your child to the people assembled, some of whom you know very well, some of whom you've never seen before, and some of whom you may never see again. Nevertheless, you are introducing your child to them, the gathered community, the Church, saying, in effect, "Church, here is our beloved daughter. Daughter, here is the Church."

Parents often think that baptism also introduces their child to God, or God to their child, but that's not the case. God already knows and loves your child, and your child already knows and loves God. You see, the two of them have been acquainted before this baptismal moment in church. "You knit me together in my mother's womb," the psalmist prays to God (Psalm 139:12, BCP). "Before I formed you in the womb I knew you," God tells the prophet Jeremiah (Jeremiah 1:5). It's an awesome thing to think about—God knowing us, loving us, calling us even before we're born into this world. But there you have it. Not only did God know and love your child before he or she was born, but God knew and loved you the same way.

That leads us to the second thing you're doing when you present your child for baptism: you're opening yourself to a spiritual encounter. Whether you've thought about it or not, choosing to have your child baptized means choosing to deepen your relationship with God. When you present your child, you also place yourself before God and the gathered community of believers. Baptism isn't simply about wanting something good for your child; it's also about wanting something good for yourself. Whether you've been part of a faith community continuously, are returning to a community you've known, or are just now entering a community with your child, when you present your child for baptism, you acknowledge in some way that God has more in store for your life as well. The Holy Spirit isn't done with your faith life.

Finally, in presenting your child, you're also choosing, in a sense, to give your child away. You're making a gift of your child to the Church. People probably don't decide to have their children baptized because they want to give them away, but that's what happens in baptism. Essentially you're saying to the gathered community, "I make a gift of this child to you." From now on there will be a connection between your child and this particular church community. That connection may be strengthened by participation in the community: worship, Sunday school, youth group. Yet even if the connection is ignored and the relationship with the community neglected, the connection is never completely severed. Adults who rarely attended church or Sunday school as children nevertheless often have a strong sense of belonging to the church in which they were baptized. In presenting your child to the Church, in making a gift of your child, you're honoring the source of all life: God. You're making a public statement that you know, at some level, that all things come from God, including your child. You're sharing the gift God has given you with the community of believers.

Receiving

So why are you giving your child to the Church? Your gift is, in a way, an exchange. You give your child in order to receive the sacrament of baptism. You want something for your child. To receive is to gain possession of something, but closed hands and hearts cannot receive. We have to be open and allow the new thing to come into our lives. To receive can also mean to act as a container. So this child you present is about to become a container for something wonderful. It's not as if your child is an empty vessel that you or the church or God is about to fill. Because of that conversation in the womb, not one of us starts life as a blank slate. But as children are baptized, they receive and are filled with living water that will nourish them for the rest of their lives. Their tiny bodies are about to embrace a sacrament.

The Sacrament of Baptism

"Sacrament" is one of those big churchy words. The catechism in The Book of Common Prayer defines a sacrament as the "outward and visible sign of inward and spiritual grace" (BCP 857). Sometime in my childhood I learned that definition by heart as a Sunday school exercise. But the phrase has resonated within me for more than thirty years and has become deeply embedded in my understanding of holiness. The sacraments stand in the area between the everyday and the divine, with one foot in each. When we talk about the sacrament of Eucharist, one of the two primary sacraments in the Anglican tradition, the bread and wine—everyday, outward, visible signs—contain, through God's action, the real presence of Christ, the body and blood of Christ. The bread and wine become holy food, and we treat them with great reverence.

In baptism, the other primary sacrament in the Anglican tradition, the outward and visible signs are the water and the oil. Again, through our prayers, these signs are imbued with the presence of the Holy Spirit, which enters those being baptized and changes their lives forever, whether they do anything about it or not. Anglicans believe that "the bond which God establishes in Baptism is indissoluble" (BCP 298). Once you have been washed with the water of baptism, the Holy Spirit can't be washed out of you. You are marked. The celebrant even says at the conclusion of the rite, "You are sealed with the Holy Spirit in Baptism and marked as Christ's own forever" (BCP 308).

At one level, of course, young children and infants have no way to say yes to this reception of the Spirit; they don't have the words for it yet. At the spiritual level, however, we believe that God and this child are already in dialogue. Thus, when a young child or infant is presented for baptism, the parents and godparents take it upon themselves to offer the child as a vessel for the Holy Spirit so the Spirit can be assimilated and welcomed with an open heart. They do this on behalf of the child, until the child can make that commitment independently.

In that one simple statement, "I present Owen to receive the Sacrament of Baptism," an entire conversation about who God is and how God acts has happened; a theological exchange has taken place. Having explored the significance of this presentation, you might think that's quite enough theology, thank you very much. But there's more to come. As in parenting, one thing leads to another. You've presented your child, but now you have some promises to make.

Getting Your Feet Wet

Things to Think About

- What does it mean for you, personally, to present your child for baptism?
- What is your own baptismal story? Who presented you for baptism?
- Why are you choosing baptism? What difference will it make for you? For your child?

Things to Try

- Write the story of your own baptism or create a baptism book using photos, your baptismal certificate, and letters from godparents.
- Begin a baptism scrapbook for your child.
- Invite your child's godparents and other family members to write letters to your child on the day of the baptism (or letters remembering the baptism). Save these letters and read them to your child on baptism anniversaries.

CHAPTER TWO

Promises, Promises!

I made several vows in regard to the way I would raise my children. I vowed I'd never serve them hot dogs, which certainly have little nutritional value and may not even really be food. I vowed I'd never buy them fast-food kids' meals that come with toys. I vowed I'd never let them watch any television shows apart from those on public broadcasting. If keeping these vows is a test of my parenting, then I've failed miserably. But when I think of the motivation behind those vows, I honestly have to say that my husband and I have done a fairly good job. In retrospect, it would have been better if I had vowed to feed my children nutritious food, to buy them thoughtful toys rather than gimmicks, and to expose them to wholesome children's programming on television. It's best to make vows about what you *will* do rather than what you *won't* do—like the vows we make on behalf of our children at baptism.

The first promises made in baptism are statements of "will do" rather than "will never do"—but they *are* a bit daunting. I truly think if parents and godparents really understood them, they'd never be able to stand up in church and make them. In fact, at baptism rehearsals, I always give the godparents a chance to back out. They never take me up on that offer. Somehow they already love their godchildren enough to promise them the moon, a promise that is just about as audacious as the baptismal promises they'll make. These promises that parents and godparents make on behalf of children can seem theologically complex and a bit overwhelming. But they're not meant to trip us up or create impossible burdens for us to carry.

In fact, Jesus promises that carrying his burden is light: "Come to me, all you that are weary and are carrying heavy burdens, and I will give you rest. Take my yoke upon you, and learn from me; for I am gentle and humble in heart, and you will find rest for your souls. For my yoke is easy, and my burden is light" (Matthew 11:28–30). Among other things, a yoke is a tool that helps you carry heavy objects. Have you ever seen a picture of someone with a wooden bar across his shoulders with a bucket attached to each side? That's one kind of yoke. If the yoke is made well, it fits you exactly and comfortably. It distributes the weight of heavy objects evenly, making them feel lighter and easier to carry. It's a matter of having the right tool. The right tool always makes the job easier. Taking on the baptismal promises is like putting on a yoke to help you with the task of parenting. The baptismal promises are meant to be helpful. They are guideposts for parents along the way.

Before our first child was born, my husband and I took parenting classes. During the first session, the teacher had us brainstorm a list of parenting goals. What did we want the outcome of our parenting to be? What attributes did we hope our child would exhibit as a result of our parenting? We'd never thought about it. The fact that we should have goals in mind and discuss them with one another was perhaps the most important thing we learned in that class. You mean there's an end result to this? It's more than working to have a good pregnancy with a healthy baby as the outcome? The list the class came up with was quite good. We hoped our children would be responsible, caring, and confident. We wanted them to grow up to be independent people, able to use their gifts and talents and act in loving ways toward themselves and others.

Baptism is about parenting within the context of a Christian life of faith. What makes this different from other parenting? Simply the fact that we want all those things on that list, and we want our child to live a life of faith as well—a life of faith within the Christian framework. What do we want for our children's faith life? The promises that come after the presentation are guidelines that help parents and godparents think about what they want as the end result of a baptized life. The parents and godparents are asked, "Will you be responsible for seeing that the child you present is brought up in the Christian faith and life?" and "Will you by your prayers and witness help this child to grow into the full stature of Christ?" (BCP 302). The parents and godparents answer, "I will, with God's help." I think the most important part of that response is the second half: "with God's help." These are weighty promises, but we don't make them in isolation, nor are we on our own to fulfill them. So the pledge is made, but just what has been promised?

"Will you be responsible for seeing that the child you present is brought up in the Christian faith and life?"

The word "responsible" comes from the same root word as "respond." It means to give an answer. You are to answer for this child. So part of what you're doing as the parent or godparent at baptism is answering for a child who is too young to answer alone and who can't yet agree to a life of faith. To be responsible also means to be trustworthy. The community is trusting that you will carry out this promise once you walk out the door of your parish church after the baptism. While the baptismal rite happens within the church, the baptismal life is lived mostly beyond the church doors. If your child is going to be brought up in the Christian faith and life, that faith and life need to be a part of everyday experience; thus, you need to be part of the community of believers. Yet attending church once a week won't give your child a faith life. Faith also needs to be lived out in the home. You child's faith formation depends, in large part, on your own example.

Maybe you, like many other parents, feel that simply raising a child is enough of a task without adding faith development to the mix. After all, keeping children fed, warm, and healthy, not to mention helping them to develop self-esteem and the skills necessary to become useful members of society, is a lot of work. But the promises you're making in the baptismal service aren't about teaching children to be useful members of society. You're promising to bring them up in the Christian faith and life. You're preparing yourself and your child to receive God's love within the framework of the Christian faith and community.

Raising a child in the Christian faith is about your life as a parent as well. It's about engaging your own faith life. Don't despair—you don't have to have a seminary degree to do this. God doesn't ask us to be successful, only faithful. What does it mean to be faithful? Sometimes people think that the opposite of faith is unbelief. But the opposite of faith is unfaith. Being unfaithful means breaking your promises, not sticking with it, not showing up. To be faithful in a marriage or partnership is to keep showing up, to stick to it even when you don't feel like it. To be faithful is to make the loving choice even when you don't feel particularly loving. As a parent, being faithful is keeping at the parenting task. And that will be easier for you if you are part of a faith community that's there to pray for and with you, to support you, and to welcome you and your child.

"Will you, by your prayers and witness, help this child to grow into the full stature of Christ?

Parenting introduces you to an entirely new layer of your vulnerabilities. This can be a good thing as well as a scary thing. Those demons you thought you had rid yourself of always seem to lurk in the background. The hard-earned patience of your adult life slips through your grasp and disappears like spilled water into the ground as your infant cries and cries and cries and refuses to be consoled. Who knew such a tiny being could challenge the forbearance of the strongest adult? Think about Jesus. He was the promised messiah, the one sent from God to save humanity and make creation new. Jesus entered the world as a human infant. I always thought it mighty audacious of God to place a newborn baby who happens to be the salvation of the world into the hands of two very new, very human parents. Just what was God thinking? New parents are much more concerned with simply keeping the baby alive than with raising the child to the full stature of Christ.

As a new mother desperate for sleep, I felt as if I nursed my infant all night long. I would sit in a chair in the wee hours, alone except for this very tiny, very vulnerable, very insatiable infant on my lap. Some nights I thought she would devour me, that I'd never make it to morning. I felt helpless, and then I felt revulsion at my helplessness. And that turned into guilt. I sat there and thought, "I have a husband who loves me, a house, food on the table, security, and I can't handle one newborn? What about all those mothers who birth their babies in poverty? I have all this support that they don't have and I can't make it through one night?" Yet somewhere under that guilt and revulsion and helplessness, a light flickered. The words of long-memorized prayers came to my lips. "Jesus Christ, Son of God, have mercy on me." "Come, let us sing to the Lord; let us shout for joy to the rock of our salvation." I couldn't manage to hold open a prayer book and keep my baby on my lap at the same time (I couldn't seem to do too many things at the same time then, but you learn), so I was stuck repeating bits of prayers and psalms I had memorized. "Lord, open our lips, and our mouths shall proclaim your praise." Months later I realized that many others had been praying for me through these difficult nights as a new mother. My own mother (a great intercessor), perhaps all mothers who had gone before, and my parish community—they were all praying for me. Just as I prayed for those mothers with fewer resources than I had, so I was held in prayer as well.

Did she see my witness, that little girl of mine? Did she feel the prayer that wrapped around both of us, kept us safe through those long dark nights? How could she not? As much as we might like to think otherwise, I believe we always communicate our most deeply held feelings and beliefs to those closest to us. And I have to believe that the flickering light cast as I threw out these lifelines somehow shielded her from the desperation that I felt. After all, we've both lived to tell the tale!

Sometimes the prayers and witness we present our children are not our best. There's nothing like being a parent to wrench at our vulnerable spots and pull them kicking and screaming into the sunlight (or the bright light of the bathroom at two in the morning as we hope there's still some children's cough medicine in the house). There have been times when my primary prayer was, "God, please make this baby stop crying." What about those times when what we witness to our children are impatience, frustration, and poor judgment? Witness? Witness me throwing a bottle across the room. Witness me saying words that my parents said to me and that I swore I'd never say to any child of mine. Witness me appeasing my toddler with more fast food and stupid toys. We can't escape the fact that we as parents are limited human beings. Our children will see—sooner rather than later—just how very human we are. In the end, our prayers and witness are made up of very ordinary and small moments. Our witness is mostly how we live every day. Our witness is how we make mistakes. And how we say we are sorry. And how we offer up the brokenness that is in us. And how we strive to become more balanced as individuals. Our children learn by watching all of these little everyday events.

Your Children Witness Too

One morning I was preparing for a funeral to be followed by an immediate departure for a weeklong conference away from home. I was all packed and, for once, had kept my usual travel anxiety at bay. I still had time to snuggle with my girls before I needed to walk out the door. I just had to pull back my hair, and I'd be ready to leave. Then my hair clip went missing. I panicked. It was my favorite one, and I was sure it had been on my dresser the night before. Suddenly the entire world seemed to conspire against me, and my well-laid plans were ruined. The stress of the upcoming day overwhelmed me, and I found myself sobbing on my bed at the unfairness of it all. The next moment two warm bodies in pajamas covered me. "It's all right, Mommy. You're going to be all right. Just take a deep breath, Mommy. That's what my teacher always says. Take a deep breath and you'll feel better."

Nothing is more powerful than being ministered to by my children. They witnessed me falling apart over a hair clip. They witnessed the pain and stress I felt at having to bury an incredible woman who had died too soon, and then to travel away from my beloved family for a week. They witnessed me being a real, vulnerable human being. And they responded with hugs and snuggles. Then they witnessed me soaking up their love, gleaning assurance from their trust that all would be well. They witnessed me drawing them close and drawing strength from their young, hopeful selves. I got my morning snuggle after all.

We won't always witness to our children the perfection we'd want them to see. We'll inevitably witness to them our frailty. And unless we're willing to get routine spiritual checkups on our own self-images and our image of God, we'll model for our children images that they will have to undo later. Actually, we'll do that anyway. We'll give our children all kinds of messages and examples that they'll have to unravel for themselves as adults. But one of the best things we can give them is a sense that as their parents, we intentionally look at our spiritual selves and keep growing. One of the best ways we can witness to our children is to say we're sorry when we've blown it as parents. We can show them what it means to ask for and accept forgiveness. We can give them the respect that we would like to receive by asking their pardon for the times we behave badly. And we can show them that we continue to grow—as parents, as individuals, as children of God.

Self-image, God-image

One fall in my parish, the Sunday school children all worked on the theme "I am a child of God." The first and second graders came out of class wearing paper medallions that they had decorated with their names and a bold proclamation: "I am Alan and I am a child of God." What a wonderful statement for parents to make and remember. What would it look like if we all wore our names on our fronts that way? "I am Anne and I am a child of God." We are all children of God with all the benefits and privileges—love, forgiveness, hope, and salvation—that come with that standing.

The more we engage with our spiritual lives as parents, the more we have to give our children. The more we work on our relationship with God, the better we are able by our prayer and witness to help them along the way of their own spiritual development. Children tend to learn from us, as well, whatever images of God we hold dear. And since many of us, consciously or unconsciously, tend to think of God as some kind of reflection of ourselves, it's important to spend some time thinking about how we image God. When was the last time you took out your image of God and looked closely at it? When was your image formed? Who most influenced it? A parent? A Sunday school teacher? A stained-glass window you sat near as a child? A picture in a book? A movie? A song? We pass on our image of God to our children. As they begin to form their own images of God, we'll have a lot of influence. If as parents we are loving and affectionate, our children will have a positive understanding of the image of God as a father or mother. If we share with them a love and reverence for nature and the outdoors, they'll gain a sense of how God is a rock. If we're joyous at mealtimes and celebrate with feasts in our home, then God's kingdom as a banquet table will be a tangible image for them. The reverse of these examples can also be true. An abusive parent leaves a child with an image of God as an abuser or harsh taskmaster. A demanding parent engenders an image of God as a deity with impossible expectations. What we do in our lives, how we approach everything, matters in the faith development of our children. We need to think about the stories we tell about heaven and God and Jesus, and the way we respond to those stories in daily living.

The Full Stature of Christ

According to the baptismal promises, the end result of our prayer and witness is to help our children attain the "full stature of Christ." Surely any parent would be comfortable promising to help a child grow. That's what being a parent means, isn't it? But who really knows what parents mean when they promise to help their child grow into the full stature of Christ? What would that look like? Your physical stature is your genetically predetermined height. Given the proper health and nourishment, children will grow to a certain height. They'll fulfill that potential for growth. Each of us has a spiritual stature as well. God gives each of us gifts we can live into. Given the proper spiritual nourishment and faith environment, a child will grow into her or his full spiritual stature. Christian parents and godparents commit themselves to a faith journey that will help their children reach their full potential: physically, emotionally, and spiritually.

This task can be quite intimidating. How can any of us reach the full stature of Christ, much less help a child get there? Again, it's helpful to remember that God doesn't ask us to be successful, only faithful, and that when we make this promise, we do so "with God's help." We're asked to try and leave the success part to God.

A friend of mine has brought her son to more than one deathbed. It started with her grandmother. When her grandmother was near death at age ninety-four, the family made a special trip to say good-bye to her. A few days later, my friend thought, "I don't think Mimi has died, and she shouldn't die alone." So she decided to make the trip again. This time she took her three-year-old son with her, because it never occurred to her not to. She woke him up from his nap and they made the trip to Mimi's place. They sang her a song and said a prayer together with a few family members. The others stepped out into the hallway, and my friend sat next to Mimi, who took her last breath while her son played on the floor. At her death, Mimi was surrounded by community. Her three-year-old great-grandson was an important part of that community. My friend witnessed many things to her son that day, not the least of which that he was a full member of the community and of his family, and that his presence was important. He wasn't kept from the deathbed, nor was he kept from his playing. At the graveside, he spontaneously began to sing again, "Jesus loves me, and he loves you too." And so the three-year-old ministered to all around him.

The bedside ministry of my friend's son didn't end there. At four, he was at his grandfather's bedside in the intensive care unit of the hospital. At five, he and his mother chanced to be at the bedside of their neighbor's mother as she died at home. He continues to sing about Jesus and God and love most days. He is well on his way to growing into the full stature of Christ. I imagine he will bring others along the way.

The promises parents and godparents make are outrageous and overwhelming and impossible to keep. But we are loved by a God who is audacious, compassionate, and unstoppable. We get a whole lot of help in fulfilling these promises, as we'll see in the next chapters.

Getting Your Feet Wet

Things to Think About

- What is the goal of your parenting? What do you want the result of your parenting to be?
- Describe your image of God. How has that image changed (or not) over the years? What experiences have most profoundly informed it?
- Who most influenced your faith life?
- Which of the baptismal promises is the most difficult for you to make on behalf of your child? Which is easiest to make? Why?

Things to Do

- Write a prayer asking God to help you with your fears about parenting.
- Talk to your parenting partner or a close friend about what kind of parent you want to be.
- Begin a parenting journal. Record your hopes, thoughts, and dreams about parenting as well as funny and poignant stories about your child that you want to remember.

CHAPTER THREE

The Answer to All Your Questions

When I was in elementary school, I sometimes attended weekday church services with one of my neighborhood friends. Her church had classes for children during their church service on Wednesday evenings. I liked going with her because the teachers there gave out candy bars if you knew the right answers to questions about Jesus and the Bible. We seldom had candy bars in my house, much less at my Sunday school, so I was impressed. I was fairly good at knowing the right answers, so I earned a good number of candy bars and looked forward to being examined about my faith by these teachers. The rewards were worth it. I was savvy enough to know that giving the answer the teacher expected was what earned me the points. I didn't always agree with their version of Jesus or God or faith. I learned something a bit different in my house and church. But I liked the candy.

In the baptismal service, we're examined about our faith too. The service includes questions for the candidates about their faith and beliefs or, when the candidates are children, questions for their parents and godparents. The reward for knowing the right answers isn't just a candy bar; it's the baptism of your child. And much more than a candy bar is at stake. As parents and godparents, you are committing your child and yourself to a lifestyle—one that includes worship services and Sunday school, picnics, prayer books, youth group, a host of potluck suppers, and faith in Jesus Christ. When you answer the questions in the examination, you're making a public statement about your faith and beliefs. The answers to the questions are fairly easy to come by—after all, they're printed in The Book of Common Prayer. But giving the answers with a sense of authenticity, placing yourself within the faith framework these questions outline, takes conscious thought.

Six questions are asked. These include three renunciations and three affirmations: three things to say no to and three things to say yes to. What you say no to is evil: spiritual, worldly, and personal. What you say yes to is Jesus Christ. The church knows better than to offer a "just say no" policy. The church is based on community, a community that knows the value of sharing burdens and being together. So in the church, after you say no, you also say yes. You get something to hold onto once you have let go of the things that get in your way.

The Renunciations

At its root, the word "renounce" means to report against someone or something. In common usage it can mean to give up or refuse. All of these meanings suggest being in relationship with someone or something to begin with, then deciding to step back, to say no, or to redirect your orientation. You can't give up something you don't have to begin with. So when we renounce something in baptism, we're saying no to something that is real and has a real pull on us.

"Do you renounce Satan and all the spiritual forces that rebel against God?"

Legend tells us that God created angels before humankind, and Lucifer was one of God's most powerful angels. His name means "light bearer," and he was one of the seraphim—the highest order of angels. But Lucifer began to yearn for more power and challenged God. So there was a war in heaven among the angels. The archangel Michael fought Lucifer and his forces and defeated them. The angels who rebelled against God were expelled from heaven. Lucifer, no longer a "light bearer," took on other names: Satan, the devil, and the tempter. So from the beginning of creation, Satan and other spiritual forces have been in rebellion against God.

It is said that one of Satan's greatest victories comes when people cease to believe in the devil. It's difficult to confront a problem if we are unable to name it. Like an illness that goes undiagnosed and so unchecked, Satan can wreak havoc in our lives if we are in denial of evil. So here, in the baptismal service, we acknowledge the power of Satan so that we can renounce it, so that we can say no to it.

What are the spiritual forces that rebel against God? Truly evil forces are at work in the universe, and we see the results of their work. I'm not talking about the possessed teenager who haunts the movie screen in horror films; I'm talking about human events that seem beyond the possible, such as the Holocaust, the genocide in Rwanda, or the corporate cover-up of chemical spills that poison the environment and kill residents through disease. I don't believe that evil can simply possess us or take over events. But I do believe that some spiritual forces lurk in the background, just waiting for an opportunity to take over chaotic human events and turn them toward evil. As parents of a young child, you may not think you'll run into any of these. But if, as parents, we are going to give our selves over to the good, if we want to be loving and make good choices for our children, we need to say no to evil and hatred and bad choices. And it's best to begin at the top—to say no to Satan and all the evil that we may not have a name for.

I think what Satan wants most is to keep any of us from being the complete person God created us to be. The spiritual forces that rebel against God try to pull us off the path toward God. When the apostle Peter tried to dissuade Jesus from the path of suffering he knew he must take, Jesus told Peter, "Get behind me, Satan!" (Matthew 16:23). These sound like harsh words from a teacher to a beloved disciple. But Jesus recognizes the evil lurking behind his friend's attempt to turn him away from his path to the cross, and he calls it as he sees it. Turning away from the path of suffering as Peter wanted him to do certainly would have been more comfortable for Jesus. But it wouldn't have been true to his calling as the messiah. It was not what the Son of God would do.

As parents, we too have to take the less comfortable path at times. For example, it's not always easy to discipline children or to teach them right from wrong. But if we step aside from this task, we raise children who are bratty and obnoxious or, worse, who have no sense of right and wrong. Then we haven't done the loving thing and we've turned away from the kind of parents we agreed to be when we promised to raise our children in the Christian faith—a faith based on love.

"Do you renounce the evil powers of this world which corrupt and destroy the creatures of God?"

For several months after my first child was born, I couldn't read the newspaper. In fact, I couldn't bear to look at the front page. The images of violence and abuse and neglect of human life that were inevitably displayed there slapped me upside the head, kicked me in the stomach, and added a kidney punch for good measure. I reeled from the pain of people worlds away from me. I seemed to have lost any buffer zone between my life and the pain of the entire world. I wanted to run and hide in my mother's arms, and I wanted to cry out in anger against the disregard for human life. It seemed that motherhood had made me at the same time both a scared child and a fierce warrior.

So I shut down and refused to look at the paper at all. The nighttime fears that accompanied my efforts to keep my tiny infant alive were enough. What did I need with the woes of the world? Yet I couldn't focus only on my child. I thought about all that I had: enough food, a warm house, and a loving husband. I thought about the medical assistance available to me and the emergency C-section that had brought my daughter safely into the world after a difficult labor. Then I thought about all the women who had less than I. Mothers who loved their newborns just as much as I loved my daughter, but who were hungry or cold or alone. Women who lacked the medical care they needed for themselves and their children. Mothers who had no access to pediatricians or infant Tylenol. Parents who were trying to raise their children in war zones.

You may think you've never run into any of the evil powers of this world. But they are there, all around us. Racism, poverty, greed, war, and addictions are all powerful forces that destroy people. They plague our communities. Take racism. It is surely evil. It's something that human beings brought into the world. It's evil because it harms people. It creates institutions and attitudes that treat some people as less than others. Knowing that every human being is created in God's image, how can we put down God's image? But we do it all the time. Poverty is another evil power of this world. We create systems that support and sustain poverty. Poverty treats some people as less than others. Much of the violence in the world comes out of the desperation of poverty. If you don't have enough to eat, then every day is a fight to stay alive. Those of us in the comfortable middle class like to say that we can't solve problems by throwing more money at them. But money is power, and if you don't have enough, life is tough.

There are subtle evils too, which play on the vulnerabilities of parents. False advertising is one. I saw it in the pamphlets that came home from the hospital with my newborn. I saw all those pictures in the parenting magazines and the pregnancy books too. The smiling mother with the beautiful baby contentedly nursing at her breast. The proud father, arms around his newly expanded family, offering peace and protection. So easy. So beautiful. Such a lie! I imagined myself on maternity leave taking long walks through parks with my baby in a stroller. What I got was barely being able to keep myself and that infant fed, much less do anything else. And I was not happy. I was depressed and scared. But I was supposed to be happy. That's what society tells you. Happy, happy, happy. Because it's supposed to be easy, easy, easy. After all, "real" mothers and fathers just know what to do. Caring for their children comes naturally.

Renouncing the evil powers of this world includes turning away from the powers that tell us we must be happy all the time. It includes saying no to the tragedies reported in the newspaper that overwhelm us. We are never parents in isolation. As parents, we respond to other parents. We grieve when we read about a four-year-old who dies at an amusement park because we imagine the loss of our four-year-old. In the nighttime, I pray, "O God, don't let any harm come to my child." In the daytime, I cry for all the children who are harmed. Does any father or mother love his or her child any less than I love mine? Does any child deserve less than mine? Do we not all desire and deserve enough food, adequate shelter, sufficient love? We can't put the good of our own children above the good of others. Yet we do it all the time. To truly renounce the evil powers of this world means to be willing to make a difference. It's about changing our perspectives and taking action to make the world a better place. Ultimately, baptism is not just about our child, but about a better life for all children.

"Do you renounce all sinful desires that draw you from the love of God?"

One summer there was a blockbuster movie that my husband and I wanted to see. Our girls were six and eight at the time; they had seen all the hype for the movie and were interested in it too. It was rated PG-13, which normally meant we wouldn't consider taking the girls to see it. But we debated this one. We wanted to go one evening on the spur of the moment, and we wanted to do something as a family rather than get a babysitter. Couldn't we take the girls to this one?

We checked out the content of the movie at a website that gives parents guidelines on such things. After reading the fine print, we decided the movie wouldn't be too scary or overwhelming for the girls. When we suggested that we go, our older daughter was adamant that she was not allowed to see PG-13 movies (see, sometimes parenting really works). But we convinced her that in this case it would be fine. We hoped it would be appropriate. And off we went.

In my hearts of hearts, I was hesitant. I knew my desire to see the movie and do it as a family outweighed my judgment about what the girls could see. And, in fact, the movie was way too scary. The girls couldn't even get through the previews without covering their eyes and holding on to us tightly. We left after the first ten minutes. My husband and I admitted it was a bad parenting choice. The girls told us in no uncertain terms that we shouldn't have taken them to see it. We went home and had ice cream and watched a silly cartoon to redeem the evening.

I certainly don't think this is the worst parenting choice we've ever made, and I give us credit for bailing when we needed to. The negative effects of our foray were short-lived. Yet we fell prey to a common parenting temptation: to do what we want to do and take our children along for the ride. Sometimes, to be the adult, we have to put our wants aside for the sake of the child. We have to say no to our own sinful desires.

In the baptismal rite, once we say no to spiritual evil and evil in the world, we then have to look at ourselves. What is it in my own life that is sinful? It's easy (and tempting) to think of sin as a list of bad things: lying, cheating, killing. But sinful desires are not always so easy to identify. Sin is about disruption in our relationship with God. We are all sinful. That is, we are all less than perfect in our relationship with God and with one another. We don't always make loving choices. Sinful desires are things that we want but that lead us away from God and from loving choices. Sinful actions are those that hurt us and others. A sinful desire could be as simple as keeping a child up way past his bedtime because we didn't want to leave our friend's house so soon. Or it could be as complicated and harmful as an addiction to alcohol. Sin draws us away from God, from love, from one another.

We never rid ourselves of sin. We always fall short of being fully the people we can be. Parenting can call us up short in many areas we thought we had conquered. It's actually a great thing for parents to have a chance to say no to these things again within the context of a celebration and a supportive community—because children can cause us to see our vulnerabilities in a whole new light, and they can teach us to love in a whole new way. Because the church intends to be a loving community, we are not left to say no to evil and stand on our own. We're given something to say yes to as well: the power of Christ. We'll explore these affirmations in the next chapter.

Getting Your Feet Wet

Things to Think About

- What pulls you off your path toward God?
- Which evil powers of this world most impact your personal life? Your faith life? Which are you called to confront?
- Which of your own personal desires is most dramatically impacted by the presence of this child in your life?
- In what ways has being a parent most challenged you so far?

Things to Do

- On your own or with your parenting partner, make a list of the activities that you will have to adjust or put aside in order to parent. Create a plan to address conflicts that may arise.
- Journal about a personal trait that you feel hinders your parenting. Explore all that this trait has taught you.
- Make a gift in your child's name to an organization that combats the evil powers of this world.

CHAPTER FOUR

We're Not Alone

A father and mother came to me concerned about their seven-year-old son. He had always been a good kid, but now that he was in grade school, things seemed to change. He became more difficult to discipline, more often defiant. I suggested they attend an upcoming parenting workshop. One of the techniques they learned there was a way of communicating their expectations to their son. It worked like magic. When their son misbehaved, they didn't merely tell him he was out of line and then punish him. Rather, they told him how they felt about his inappropriate actions and what they expected of him. They still followed up with a logical consequence when he misbehaved, but by naming his actions and pointing him in the right direction, they gave him the tools he needed to improve his behavior. The results were immediate and very gratifying. The defiance disappeared almost overnight. Their son still misbehaved from time to time, as all of us do. But they now had a method and a plan to address their concerns.

The Affirmations: Turning to God

None of us is perfect. But just as those parents discovered a valuable tool to assist them in helping their son get back on the right track, all through our lives, we too can turn to God and our faith community when we're ready to turn away from bad choices. That's what the three renunciation questions in the service of baptism are all about. These questions are followed by three affirmations or "yes" questions. They give us something positive to turn to.

"Do you turn to Jesus Christ and accept him as your Savior?"

When we turn our backs on Satan, we turn toward Jesus Christ. After all, being a Christian means being a follower of Christ. Who do you turn to? In times of stress and trouble, who do you turn to? Relationships are what give us life. The parenting relationship is what brings you to this baptismal examination. So as a parent, who do you turn to when times are tough? Someone you know will help you no matter what. Someone who doesn't judge you when you are at your worst. Someone who won't make you pay for it later. Someone you can trust to see you at the bottom. Someone who has been to the bottom too and knows the way out.

But it's not only in times of desperation that we turn to others. We also seek out relationships in times of joy. Who do you turn to in times of joy and celebration? Someone who will delight in your gifts. Someone who isn't envious or competitive. Someone who knows you well enough to understand your joy. Someone who will rejoice with you. Someone who knows what it is to be joyful. Someone who will laugh with you, dance with you, sing with you with abandon.

The point of being a Christian, of believing in Christ, is trusting that Christ is the someone we can turn to. We can turn to Jesus Christ in times of trouble and in times of joy; Christ is the one who will be with us. Christ is the one who has endured human suffering and who can complete our joy. When Jesus sat with his friends around the dinner table, teaching them about God's promises and love, he said to them, "I have said these things to you so that my joy may be in you, and that your joy may be complete" (John 15:11). Jesus wants us to be filled with joy.

To say, "Yes, I turn to Jesus Christ," is to say, "Yes, I know that there lies my hope." We call Jesus our savior. Simply put, a savior is one who saves. Jesus Christ saves us by knowing us better than anyone else. Just as the best of friends saves us in times of trouble by being the person we can turn to, so Christ saves us, in the worst of times and in the best of times. To accept Jesus Christ as our savior is to be willing to believe that Christ knows and loves us and is always standing by us. Whether we know it or not, whether we are willing to accept it or not, Christ holds out loving arms to enfold us in an embrace. To turn to Jesus Christ as our savior is to be willing to consider the possibility that through Christ's death and resurrection, we are somehow already saved, that nothing the world dishes out can ultimately destroy us. In the here and now, Christ stands with us in the pain and in the joy. Christ is ready for us, waiting for us to turn and say, "Yes!" The most amazing thing of it all is that whether we say yes or not, Christ continues to love us. Whether we accept it or not, Christ's hand is held out to pull us out of the dark water of fear and death and into the light of joy and life.

There's another great benefit to saying yes to Christ after saying no to Satan. The minute we say yes to Jesus Christ, we admit that we aren't in this life alone. And that gives us the power to go on.

"Do you put your whole trust in his grace and love?"

Once we've said yes and turned our hearts to Christ, there's nothing for it but to put our whole trust in his grace and love. This affirmation can be paired with the renunciation of worldly evil. We say no to evil and yes to love. Grace and love are what combat evil. Notice we are asked to place our trust not in Christ's power or dominion, not in rules and regulations, but in grace, which pours out on us without our having to earn it, and in love, which is the greatest power of all. When we place our trust in Christ's grace and love, we put our trust in this truth: God loves us, and through Christ we are pulled into the love of God. We do this so that when we fail as parents, we know it doesn't end there. We have a wall of strength behind us in Christ's grace and love to fall back on. We don't have to be destroyed by our mistakes. Our children don't have to be destroyed by our mistakes. We are not in this life alone.

The story is told about a man who placed his trust in God and never doubted that God would save him. One day a great flood rushed through his town and threatened his house. As his neighbors scrambled into their car to evacuate, they noticed him sitting on his porch. They called to him, offering to take him to safety in their car. "I'm fine," he replied. "I trust that God will save me." So they left without him. Soon the floodwaters rose, and the man had to move to a second-story balcony. A police boat came by, and the officers on board asked him to jump in. "No thanks," said the man. "I trust that

God will save me." So the boat cruised on. Finally the man was forced to climb on top of his roof as the floodwaters rose higher. A rescue helicopter came by and lowered a rope for him. But the man refused to climb up the rope. "I trust that God will save me!" he yelled to the rescuers. They had to leave without him. The floodwaters rose and the man drowned. When he came face-to-face with God, the man was angry. "God, I was faithful my whole life. I trusted that you would save me. Why didn't you?" God looked at the man and said, "I sent you a car, a boat, and a helicopter. What more did you need?" When we rest our backs against the wall of Christ's love, we find that God's help is all around us. Often God works through others to help us through difficult times. When it comes to parenting, it's good news indeed that we don't have to trust only in our own limited resources.

My husband was the one to suggest we take parenting classes before our first daughter was born. He was enamored of our friends' two-year-old and thought they were amazing parents. They had taken this parenting class. A parenting class? The thought hadn't occurred to me. But it made so much sense. When I wanted to learn to sing, I took voice lessons. To learn to preach, I took preaching classes. Surely parenting was even more important. So we went, and we were the only pregnant couple in the class. It was transforming. Not only did we learn a lot about parenting (we had to practice on our cats and the youth group at church, not having our own child yet), we learned a lot about ourselves, our expectations of each other, and our vision of the result of our parenting. Ten years later, we continue to use skills and wisdom we gained in that class.

Placing our trust in the grace and love of Christ means that we can always be on the lookout for a helping hand. It means that when we're tired or overwhelmed or confused or angry or at the end of our ropes, we have a place to lay ourselves down and cry if we need to. We can rest in the arms of Christ and trust in not one thing, but two: grace and love. What does grace look like? Taste like? Feel like? What does it mean to have the grace of Christ given to us as parents? Grace is sometimes described as undeserved forgiveness. When we make mistakes as people, as parents, we can trust that Christ forgives us. Forgiveness is an action. It's a way that Christ acts toward us. The funny thing is that it doesn't depend on our actions at all. It doesn't depend on our asking for or accepting the forgiveness. It doesn't even depend on our acknowledgment of our failures. That's hard to believe, especially when we feel that we've failed or that we should have done better. But Christ forgives us whether we're aware of it or not.

To trust in Christ's grace is to be able to relax into the truth that we won't be held in contempt for our failings. Rather, we'll be held in love. It's a hard thing for us to believe: so much of what we're taught about failure and forgiveness leads us to think that we have to deserve forgiveness. My father used to tell us that he was thankful that God treated us with mercy rather than as we deserved. We don't receive grace and love because we deserve them or have somehow earned them; we receive them because God delights in us and wants to give us good things. Jesus says, "Is there anyone among you who, if your child asks for a fish, will give a snake instead of a fish? Or if the child asks for an egg, will give a scorpion?" (Luke 11:11–12). Jesus goes on to say that if we, as limited human beings who don't always get it right, know how to give good gifts to our children, doesn't our Father in heaven know how to do it even better?

That's really the only way we can be loving parents. We have to put our trust somewhere, and if we trust only in ourselves, we'll lose it in the middle of the night. We'll fail. We'll make big mistakes. If we put our whole trust in Christ, we'll still lose it in the middle of the night, we'll still fail, and we'll still make big mistakes. But when we do, the grace and love of Christ are waiting there to catch us. We are not alone. The promise of Jesus, who suffered on the cross, is that there is no dark place in human experience that Christ hasn't walked before us or won't walk with us. Nowhere we can go, in heaven or hell, is beyond God's presence and God's love for us. The psalmist sings to God:

> Where can I go then from your Spirit?
>
> > where can I flee from your presence?
>
> If I climb up to heaven, you are there;
>
> > if I make the grave my bed, you are there also.
>
> If I take the wings of the morning
>
> > and dwell in the uttermost parts of the sea,
>
> Even there your hand will lead me,
>
> > and your right hand hold me fast.
>
> (PSALM 139:6–9, BCP)   .

Parenting can deliver us to unexpected highs and devastating lows in the matter of a few moments. It's good to know we are in safe hands—God's hands—all along the way.

Once, in the middle of the night, I sat with my firstborn, absolutely sure I couldn't do it. I couldn't possibly make it as a parent. I didn't know what I was going to do. She wasn't even a month old, and already I had failed to keep her fed, content, and happy at all times. I had smashed her finger in a door. I couldn't nurse her efficiently enough, and she was losing weight. I was so exhausted all the time that I never had energy to sing to her or smile or do any of those things parents are supposed to do. How awful it was! But how much worse it would have been if I'd thought that was it, that there was no place for me to turn. If I'd thought my failure as a parent was my daughter's entire story, I'd have been utterly lost. I cried that night. I cried a lot of nights. I cried out to God long and hard and often. I clutched for that hand in the middle of the night, and despair did not win. I wept on the phone to friends who were too far away to see in person and made it through another day. I waited anxiously by the front door in the evening, willing my husband to come home before I dropped that baby and ran. And he always did. He held that baby. He held me. And we muddled through.

We will fail in our parenting. But these failures will not be the end of our story as parents to our children, or as children to God.

"Do you promise to follow and obey him as your Lord?"

"I have decided to follow Jesus, no turning back, no turning back," so goes the song. If only it were that easy. I've never understood why it is that once I've figured out that trusting in God really does make things work better, I can't seem to just do it. Why is living a life of faith so difficult? Perhaps this is why the word "promise" begins this question. I have to make a commitment to follow and obey, and it won't always be easy.

We are automatically God's children through our own baptisms. In baptism, "God adopts us as his children" (BCP 858). God calls us into a loving relationship, a relationship to which God is always faithful. But we are not so constant. To be faithful to that relationship is a choice we have to make again and again. We're not on automatic pilot when it comes to following Jesus.

What kind of relationship would that be, one in which we had no choice but to follow and obey? Rather, we're in the driver's seat when it comes to following our Lord. So we make a promise, a commitment. We bind ourselves to the one who gives us life. For us, being faithful to God is a choice. The truth is, if we follow and obey Christ, we won't get off course. After all, we ask the same things of our children. We expect them to follow and obey us.

My oldest daughter was two when my second daughter was born. I thought I'd learned to multitask with one child; two children gave me a very steep learning curve indeed. When my younger daughter was just a few weeks old, I ventured out with both children to a mothers' meeting and playgroup. I managed to pack a diaper bag for two, bring the necessary snack items, and wrestle each of them into the appropriate car seat. We arrived at our destination, and I parked along the city street in front of my friend's home. Then the next challenge presented itself. Which child do I unbuckle first? Do I let the toddler out and leave her to her own devices as I struggle to wrest the infant car seat from the car? Or do I set the baby alone on the sidewalk while I coax the toddler out of her seat as efficiently as possible? It may not seem like such a dilemma in retrospect, but at the time I was daunted. I chose to unleash the toddler first. This is where that follow and obey stuff comes in handy.

I had to know that on a busy city street, she would follow my directions and obey my instructions. "You must stand on the sidewalk next to the car," I directed her. "You may not under any circumstances run around the car. This is a busy street, and I want you to be safe. Mommy can't hold your hand just yet—she's busy getting your sister out of the car." We managed. We stayed safe and arrived at our destination. As my children age, the situations they face that threaten their safety become more complex. And as they grow, they have the power to make devastating choices. My concern that they follow my directions remains. I won't always be there to guide them. I hope to instill in them some internal guidance along the way. Obeying is as much about love as it is about safety.

For us as parents, then, obeying Christ is also about love. In a real sense, choosing to be faithful children to God helps us to be faithful parents to our children. We want our children to turn to us in pain and in joy. We tell them they can trust us, at least trust in our love if not always our patience. We do want them to follow and obey us, so we'd better know just where we're lead-

ing them. In the Christian life, there's one sure way to know that we are leading our children on the path of life: keeping ourselves on the path that God
lays before us. How do we know this path? It's not always easy. But then
again, we're not left without a guide. To obey Christ, we need to know what
Christ teaches. For that we have scripture, the wisdom of the church, and the
experience of Christian community.

These renunciations and promises of the baptismal service are the foundation on which we can become the best parents God created us to be. We
sort out our own spiritual lives so that we can get on with the mighty work
of loving and lending a hand in the formation of our children, not only as
loving adults, but as loving Christians as well.

Parenting in Community

About a week before she was due, a friend of mine was in church, and at the
end of the service, a man sitting behind her said, "I sat behind the most
beautiful woman in the world today." She looked at him somewhat incredu-
lously, and he explained that he felt that pregnant women radiated beauty as
they carried new life within them. What a difference that made to her, feeling huge and uncomfortable and unattractive as one does when near to giving birth. When her son was baptized in that parish a few weeks later, she
realized how much the support of her Christian community meant to her.
Just a word of encouragement from a stranger can make all the difference.
Every time she witnesses a baptism, she is reminded of the generations who
have passed down the faith, and of the importance of keeping that faith.

It's because we are serious about the support of the Christian community
that, in the Episcopal Church, we baptize people in the middle of a typical
Sunday service. In fact, the baptismal directions in The Book of Common
Prayer state that the sacrament of Holy Baptism is to be administered during the main Eucharist on a Sunday or other major feast (BCP 298). Because
baptism welcomes the child into the church community, the community
needs to be present. For most parishes, the Sunday morning Eucharist is the
time when the community is most itself.

Once, at a baptism rehearsal, I asked a group of parents and godparents
what they wanted their child to gain from baptism. One of their responses

was, "an extended family." I was delighted by this response, because that is exactly one of the things that happens. After all those being baptized have been presented and the promises have been made by parents and sponsors, the members of the congregation are asked for their support. "Will you who witness these vows," says the celebrant, addressing the congregation, "do all in your power to support these persons in their life in Christ?" (BCP 303). Everyone there—those who know the individuals about to be baptized and those who have never seen them before, those who are serious about their own faith and those who are just visiting, those who are paying attention and those who are not—everyone is included.

Once again, the importance of witness is emphasized. Now, rather than the parents and godparents witnessing to beloved children, the members of the congregation witness the vows. Like the old debate about whether a tree falling in the forest, with nobody there to hear it, really does make a sound, we ask, are vows made without anyone to witness them really vows? The congregation is there to help the parents and godparents remember what they said they would do. This witness gives the vows power.

The congregation makes a promise too. The members promise to do all in their power "to support these persons in their life in Christ." Who are "these persons" the members promise to help? They are the sponsors as well as the candidates. The congregation promises to support the parents and godparents as well as the children about to be baptized.

So how do they help? Where are these persons at one in the morning when the infant is crying inconsolably, or the four-year-old has wet the bed, or the teenager isn't yet home? Well, they may be asleep or at work or worrying about their own teenager. But they're also a part of your Christian community. They may be the usher who makes your child feel welcome in church, or the Sunday school teacher who tells your child Bible stories, or the nursery volunteer who watches your child so you can worship, or the youth leader who will take your teenager on a pilgrimage, or a member of the prayer group who prays for you when you least suspect it but most need it. Who knows? Even when these members of the congregation make these promises, they have no idea how they may interact with your child from that day forward. It takes a lot of faith. It takes God.

In one congregation I served, the teenagers went on a ten-day pilgrimage as part of their two-year confirmation preparation. Adults other than their parents were the chaperones and mentors on that journey, which took them far from home. The youth gained faithful adult companions on their faith journey. The adults gained faithful youth companions on their faith journey. It was a win-win situation. Many lasting friendships were formed. The year after one such pilgrimage, two of the adult chaperones lost their mothers within a week of each other. What struck me was how the youth who had been on that pilgrimage reached out to the two women who were grieving. These young people made a point of attending the funerals, some serving as acolytes. In one case it meant driving an hour to a different church on a Saturday morning. But they came.

I don't know if those two women were in the congregation the day any of those youth were baptized. If they had been, they couldn't have known that some years later they would minister to those youth on a pilgrimage. Nor could they have known that those same youth would minister to them in a time of loss and grief. But that's what a faith community does. That's the kind of support the members of a congregation offer when they witness the baptismal vows. They promise to be there in unexpected ways at unexpected times. They promise to be part of the larger faith community that surrounds and supports the parents, godparents, and children.

Supportive communities don't always see us at our best. Part of what makes them supportive is that their care for us isn't dependent on our being at our best. It's actually very brave of parents to submit themselves to such a public event as baptism, a highly charged, emotional event bound to set adults and infants alike on edge. It's almost guaranteed that somebody will cry, and it might well be one of the adults! A woman I know—and greatly respect for her wise outlook and calm approach to life—remembers being deeply embarrassed at the baptism of her first child. Her son, who up to this point had seemed such a lovely and docile child, wailed and wailed and wailed through the entire baptismal service. She just knew the congregation recognized how unskilled she was at this mothering job. She could hear the unspoken comments—"Can't she keep that baby quiet?" Afterward, an older woman approached her. She took the boy's tiny hand in her gnarled fingers and smiled. "Did you know," she asked, "that when a baby cries at his baptism, it's the devil coming out? You should have smooth sailing from now on." It's this kindness that lingers with the mother rather than the fear and embarrassment. Twenty-five years later, she thinks of how she might pass on this kindness to another young mother uncertain of her skills.

So the children have been presented, the parents and godparents have made promises and been examined, and the congregation has made a formal pledge to help. The players are all present and the baptismal font stands ready. Yet before anyone enters those waters, it's good to remember just who you are involving with all these pledges. It's time to look at our relationship with God as outlined in the Baptismal Covenant.

Getting Your Feet Wet

Things to Think About

- What feeds your faith?
- In what ways have you experienced Christ's love enfolding you? Have you known God's saving grace through people or circumstances?
- If you could design a class on raising children in the Christian faith, what topics would you include?

Things to Do

- Make a list of all the people who support you as a parent: your church, your family, your friends. Write a prayer asking God to support the people who support you in parenting.
- Take some quiet time by yourself and think about your renewed promise to turn to Jesus Christ as your savior. Choose one thing that feeds your faith (such as going to church, quiet prayer time at home, spiritual reading, helping others), and decide how you might wrap that into your life as a parent.

CHAPTER FIVE

The Baptismal Covenant

Early in my ordained ministry, I remember being surprised when a parishioner told me how much he loved baptism services. I guess I had been more attuned to the folks who sighed with resignation when they walked into church on a Sunday morning and realized there was going to be a baptism that day. To them, this meant a longer-than-usual service honoring a family they didn't really know. They felt unconnected. But this man responded to baptisms with great enthusiasm. He said that when the congregation joined in reciting the baptismal covenant, he felt excited about remembering his own baptism and that of his son, now a teenager. I remember thinking at the time, "He really gets it!"

Up to this point in the service, the congregation has taken on the role of witness. That role changes now as every baptized member is asked to renew her or his own baptism through the Baptismal Covenant. The focus widens from the individual candidates and their sponsors to include the entire gathered community. Through reciting the Baptismal Covenant, the members of the congregation renew their own baptisms.

A covenant is a formal agreement. A covenant with God is sacred and binding. One of our basic understandings about God is that God has made an unbreakable covenant with God's people. God has pledged God's self to us and claimed us as God's people. As the psalmist says, "For he is our God, and we are the people of his pasture, and the sheep of his hand" (Psalm 95:7, BCP). Scripture is full of stories about specific covenants God made with specific people. One of the earliest was Noah.

The Noah story is a wonderful baptismal story. After all, it involves water, new birth, and a covenant between God and creation. I sometimes wonder whether the Noah story isn't the most used biblical story in our culture. It's easy to find everything from crib sheets to curtains to wallpaper emblazoned with Noah's ark. Bookstores abound with beautifully illustrated versions of the story. Secular stores sell many toy versions of Noah's ark. We have at least three in our house, and I remember playing a beloved Noah's ark board game as a kid. Yet when I ask families to recall the Noah story during baptismal instruction, few of them really remember the details. They remember that God told Noah to build an ark, that the animals were placed in the ark (usually people remember two by two) and that it rained (usually people remember that it rained for forty days and nights). That's about it. But even this slim outline tells us that the Noah story is an important story about rebirth. Noah gathers two of every animal, one male and one female, and places them in the ark. Noah is joined by his wife and their three sons and their wives. So within the ark is all that is necessary for creation to be fruitful and multiply. Then this vessel, full of the possibility of new life, is surrounded and carried by water for forty days and nights. The number forty is significant. Not only is it repeated in several biblical accounts (Moses and the people wandered for forty years, Jesus was tempted in the desert for forty days); it also happens to correspond to human pregnancy: women carry their children in the womb, surrounded by water, for forty weeks.

So the Noah story is literally one about new birth. As the floodwaters recede and the ark comes to halt on dry ground, Noah and his family and the creatures disembark to repopulate the earth. But there is more. They also begin a new life and a new covenant relationship with God. One of the details people tend to miss in recalling this story is the rainbow. The rainbow is a significant aspect of this covenant story. Once Noah, his family, and all of the creatures are safe on dry land, Noah builds an altar and gives thanks to God. God responds with a gift for Noah. God says to Noah, "As for me, I am establishing my covenant with you and your descendants after you," and God goes on to promise that never again will a flood destroy the earth. God says, "This is the sign of the covenant that I make between me and you and every living creature that is with you, for all future generations: I have set my bow in the clouds, and it shall be a sign of the covenant between me and the earth." God goes on to say that whenever we see a rainbow, we will remember these words and the covenant (Genesis 9:8–17). This covenant is integral to the new creation, the rebirth that is accomplished by Noah's faithfulness.

Our rite of baptism is also about rebirth and faithfulness. Like Noah and generations of people who have come before us, we understand ourselves as

God's people. In the Episcopal Church we express our relationship with God through the Baptismal Covenant. When we as the church renew our Baptismal Covenant with God, we are remembering our baptisms and recalling the agreement that is made in baptism. Through baptism we are marked as belonging to Christ forever. For our part in the agreement, we promise to renounce evil and follow Jesus as our savior. God promises to free us from sin and death.

The Baptismal Covenant is also about love. It encompasses our loving relationship with God that is represented in the church's creeds or statements of belief. In the Anglican tradition, we hold to two main creeds: the Nicene Creed and the Apostles' Creed. We recite the Nicene Creed as part of our Sunday eucharistic worship. The Apostles' Creed, which came out of early baptismal examinations, is said during Morning or Evening Prayer. Our current Baptismal Covenant begins with the Apostles' Creed, put once again into question and answer form.

The Baptismal Covenant

Celebrant Do you believe in God the Father?
People I believe in God, the Father almighty,
             creator of heaven and earth.

Celebrant Do you believe in Jesus Christ, the Son of God?
People I believe in Jesus Christ, his only Son, our Lord.
             He was conceived by the power of the Holy Spirit
                and born of the Virgin Mary.
             He suffered under Pontius Pilate,
                was crucified, died, and was buried.
             He descended to the dead.
             On the third day he rose again.
             He ascended into heaven,
                and is seated at the right hand of the Father.
             He will come again to judge the living and the dead.

Celebrant Do you believe in God the Holy Spirit?
People I believe in the Holy Spirit,
             the holy catholic Church

the communion of saints,
the forgiveness of sins,
the resurrection of the body,
and the life everlasting. (BCP 304)

The word "creed" comes from the Latin word "credo," which means "I believe." Indeed, both the Nicene Creed and the Apostles' Creed are statements of belief. In this part of the Baptismal Covenant, we state just what we believe about God and Jesus and the Holy Spirit. As a statement of belief, the creed is both easy and difficult to understand. In a few words, early church teachers tried to express eternal truth about God. We could spend much time talking about just what the creed means. But that would be only one way of understanding it. We also engage our hearts when we pledge ourselves to God. A colleague of mine says we should "think of the creed not simply as a work of the mind but as a matter of the heart. The true meaning of believing, in spirit and in truth, is one of setting one's heart on, giving one's heart to."[5] You've already given your heart to this beloved child whom you've brought to the church for baptism. My friend goes on to suggest that what we do in the creed is give our hearts to God. Instead of saying, "I believe in God, the Father almighty . . . ," we might just as well say, "I have given my heart to God, the Father almighty. I have given my heart to Jesus Christ. I have given my heart to the Holy Spirit."

Thus, reciting the first part of the Baptismal Covenant is not only a rehearsal of the basic tenets of our faith; it is also an opportunity to realign ourselves in our relationship with God, to set our hearts in the right place.

Having aligned ourselves again with the God who loved us into being, we're now ready to enact our love. The second part of the baptismal covenant consists of five promises that represent what it means to live a baptized life. In early Anglican tradition, baptismal candidates were asked if they would keep God's holy will and commandments.[6] What can we do to keep God's holy will and commandments? The five questions at the end of the baptismal covenant give us an outline of what we can do.

Celebrant   Will you continue in the apostles' teaching and fellowship,
in the breaking of bread, and in the prayers?

People   I will, with God's help.

Celebrant	Will you persevere in resisting evil, and, whenever you fall into sin, repent and return to the Lord?
People	I will, with God's help.
Celebrant	Will you proclaim by word and example the Good News of God in Christ?
People	I will, with God's help.
Celebrant	Will you seek and serve Christ in all persons, loving your neighbor as yourself?
People	I will, with God's help.
Celebrant	Will you strive for justice and peace among all people, and respect the dignity of every human being?
People	I will, with God's help. (BCP 304–5)

The Baptismal Covenant is about remembering our baptisms. Now, if you were baptized as an infant, you may say that you can't possibly remember your baptism. But I'm talking about more than memory. To remember is to "re-member"—to pull the members back together. In the case of baptism in the church, re-membering is a collective action. The community members are gathered together on a Sunday morning and become more fully the body of Christ. Dispersed through the week, when they gather to celebrate baptism and Eucharist, they have re-membered. In the same way, to re-member our baptisms is to gather together all the parts of what it means to be baptized and consciously think about them.

These five promises give us explicit guidelines for how to live a baptized life. In part 2 of this book, we'll look closely at each of the promises and how we can live them out in the household each day. These promises are helpful not only to parents and households, but also to the church community as a whole. The Baptismal Covenant instructs the entire congregation in how it can go about its ministry, how it can most be the body of Christ. As members of the body of Christ, we're called to be Christ's ambassadors in the world and to minister in the name of Christ. We are called to feed the hungry, clothe the naked, and heal the sick. We are called to love our enemies and neighbors, work for justice, and be people of peace. The Baptismal Covenant shows us how to do this. It's a teaching tool as well as a pledge.

In the baptismal service, the proclamation of the Baptismal Covenant is followed by a short litany called "Prayers for the Candidates." These prayers are wonderful petitions for those about to enter the Christian faith and life. They're quite assertive—they ask God to deliver, open, fill, keep, teach, send, and bring. They don't assume that the candidates know all there is to know about the Christian faith and life and thus may now be admitted to the community. Rather, they assert that by entering into the baptismal waters, the candidates will receive the sacrament of new birth and begin a wondrous journey of discovery of the Christian life and faith. Along the way, God will deliver them from sin, open their hearts, fill them with new life, keep them safe, teach them to love, send them to witness, and bring them into God's peace. It's really a pretty good deal.

Getting Your Feet Wet

Things to Think About

- What can you give your heart to?
- Do you believe all of the tenets of the faith that are affirmed in the Baptismal Covenant? Which ones are you most comfortable with? Which ones raise questions for you?
- What effect does each baptismal service in which you participate have on your own baptismal story?
- Which of the prayers for the candidates (BCP 305) most clearly articulates your own prayers for your child's life in Christ?

Things to Do

- Read the Noah story (Genesis 6:11–22; 7:11–24; 8:6–18; 9:8–17) and notice how many times the word "covenant" is used. Find an illustrated version of the story to read with your child, and talk about the symbolism of the rainbow as a sign of God's covenant or promise (try Jan Brett's *On Noah's Ark*).
- Write your own creed. What do you most believe about God?

CHAPTER SIX

The Baptism

As a child, I was baptized in a small Episcopal church when I was a month old. The priest poured water over my head from a stone font while my parents, godparents, and other family stood by. I am assured it was a fine day. But I had another sort of baptism at the age of two that was not so fine. My family was traveling and had stopped at a hotel for the night. We all went to the pool for a refreshing swim before dinner. My father had gone back to the hotel room to change for dinner, and my mother was trying to entice me into the shallow end, but I refused to touch the water.

Then she noticed my two older brothers in the deep end, diving off the board into an inner tube. Concerned that they were out of their depth (so to speak), she left me sitting on the side and swam the length of the small pool to move the boys into a safer zone. She turned around only to see that I was no longer on the side of the pool, but well on my way to the bottom of it. At that instant, my father appeared dressed for dinner. At her yell, he went in after me, clothes and all. Apparently he had to dry out the money from his wallet before we could go to dinner. A terrifying moment and memory for my parents, but we've all lived to tell the tale. Water is a powerful force, dangerous as well as life giving.

Thanksgiving over the Water

If I invited parents and godparents to bring their beloved children to the church on such and such a day so that we could drown them, everyone would be horrified. Yet that is, in part, what we're doing. As the ritual finally moves to the font, the "Thanksgiving over the Water" is prayed. Through giving thanks, this prayer blesses the water that will shortly be poured over the candidates in baptism. Water: powerful, cleansing, life giving. The water is blessed, but it's really the water that blesses *us*. In all of God's creation, water is unique—it's the only element found naturally as a solid, liquid, and gas. Oceans cover almost three-quarters of the earth's surface, and water comprises half to three-quarters of our bodies. We can't live without it. In this prayer, the water stories of our faith are remembered, starting with its presence and power at the beginning of creation. We remember the waters of the deep over which the Holy Spirit moved when God created the world. We remember the water of the Red Sea through which Moses led God's people to freedom. We remember the water of the Jordan River in which John baptized Jesus. We remember that water brings death as well as life and that we are about to drown the candidates in order to give them new life.

The prayer says it. We intend, through baptism, to bury these children with Christ in his death. Rebirth, after all, doesn't happen without death. Do you remember the first time you ever planted a seed? I still remember the cut-off pint-sized milk cartons in my kindergarten class. Small pudgy fingers poked a hole in the damp soil, into which a seed was dropped. The cartons were carefully watered and set on the classroom windowsill to soak up the sunshine. And we waited. As patiently as only five-year-olds can, we waited for the miracle. And after an unbelievably long time, it happened. A green shoot pushed itself up out of the dirt. Water had worked its miracle, splitting open the husk around the seed and releasing the new growth.

Jesus said, "Very truly, I tell you, unless a grain of wheat falls into the earth and dies, it remains just a single grain; but if it dies, it bears much fruit" (John 12:24). We bring these children to the font to die that they might live. We drown them in the baptismal waters to unleash the miracle within, the miracle of who they are, the potential to grow into the full stature of Christ.

The Baptism

So all has been prepared; all is ready. The ancient formula is about to be reenacted once again. The powerful name of the Trinity will be invoked. Simple water will be used. Whether from a river or a font or a puddle on the side of the road, it doesn't matter. Each candidate is presented by name to the celebrant, who immerses each body or pours water over each head, saying, "Taylor, I baptize you in the name of the Father and of the Son and of the Holy Spirit." The uniqueness of each person is honored by the use of his or her name. The continuity of the rite and the teaching of Jesus are honored by the use of the ancient invocation of the Trinity. And everyone says amen. "Amen" is the liturgical word of affirmation. It means "so be it" in Hebrew. Thus, the gathered community gives its consent for, and celebrates the receiving of, this new member into the body. The baptism itself is brief compared to what has already taken place. But the preparation is necessary to create the fertile soil in which this new life in Christ can thrive. The foundation is as important as the moment itself.

When I was still in seminary, one of my classmates brought his daughter to be baptized in the seminary chapel. There was no permanent font in the chapel, no standard carved stone fixture presented years before as a memorial to someone. Rather, a large copper trough was brought out for the occasion and placed in the center of the aisle. When the moment came, the baby girl was undressed and entirely immersed in the trough. She came up wet, red, and screaming. Her mother quickly bundled her into a clean diaper and white christening gown. The symbolism was impossible to miss. This girl, born only weeks before, was sent once more into the water of the womb and brought again to life, wet, red, and screaming, to be placed into the hands of her loving parents, who in turn were held in the arms of the community, which was itself held in God's loving embrace.

In the early days of the church, the apostle Philip baptized a man in some water by the side of the road. Sometimes I imagine this water as a roadside puddle. An angel had sent Philip on a trip down a wilderness road, for no stated reason. But along this road Philip met a man from Ethiopia, a high-ranking official from the court of the queen. This man happened to be reading from the Hebrew Scriptures, the prophet Isaiah, to be exact. Soon Philip was seated beside him in the chariot, and "starting with this scripture, he proclaimed to him the good news about Jesus." The Ethiopian noticed water alongside the road and asked to be baptized then and there. Philip willingly complied; the man was baptized and went on his way rejoicing (Acts 8:26–40). There was very little ritual. Rather, there was instruction in scripture, a stated desire to be baptized, and the necessary water. These are the elements needed to begin a new life in Christ.

Chrismation

If you take a close look at all of the instruction surrounding the actual baptismal service, you'll notice a preference for the bishop to lead the service and perform the baptisms. That's because in the early church, each community was headed by a bishop, assisted by deacons. The order of presbyters (or priests) came along later as the church grew too big for each bishop to meet regularly with the worshiping communities. Still today, any priest or deacon who performs a baptism does so on behalf of the bishop. The oil of chrism used at baptism is a mark of the bishop's presence even when the bishop isn't physically present.

The oil of chrism is oil that has been blessed by the bishop specifically for baptism. The oil is used to seal the baptism. The tradition of anointing with oil is an ancient one. Oil was used to anoint kings, heal sicknesses, and prepare bodies for burial. Each of these symbols is present in the baptism. Through baptism the candidates are prepared for burial, offered healing, and named as heirs of God's kingdom. Once someone has been baptized with water, the baptism is sealed with chrism, the presider saying, "Taylor, you are sealed with the Holy Spirit in Baptism and marked as Christ's own forever." When present, the bishop makes the sign of the cross on each newly baptized forehead with the oil of chrism. When the bishop isn't present, the priest does this instead, but through the use of the chrism, the presence of the bishop is called to mind. This present-day connection to the bishop connects each of the newly baptized all the way back to that early church—to Philip and the Ethiopian, to Peter and Paul, each of whom was filled with the Holy Spirit. And through the tradition of the church, the hands of those apostles were laid on the heads of those they taught, who in turn laid their hands on other heads, who passed on the tradition to this very day, to our own bishops who had hands laid on them. These hands and all the hands before them are the hands that bless the chrism.

So much has happened in the space of less than an hour in the life of an infant and her or his parents. And as the baptismal ritual comes to a close, two final things happen: gifts and reception.

Baptismal Gifts

At the party in our house after our older daughter's baptism, her godfather, a Benedictine monk, looked at the shelf holding some of her gifts and remarked, "Not many month-old infants have their own chapel!" There on the shelf were a copy of *The Book of Common Prayer*, given by her godmother; an icon of Jesus that her godfather had written; and her baptismal candle. What else would a new Christian need?

The church also gives baptismal gifts. They are found in the collect that is prayed over people after they have been baptized:

> *Heavenly Father, we thank you that by water and the Holy Spirit you have bestowed upon these your servants the forgiveness of sin, and have raised them to the new life of grace. Sustain them, O Lord, in your Holy Spirit. Give them an inquiring and discerning heart, the courage to will and to persevere, a spirit to know and to love you, and the gift of joy and wonder in all your works. Amen. (BCP 308)*

Having welcomed these new Christians, we immediately ask God to bestow gifts on them: a discerning heart, courage, a loving spirit, joy and wonder. What wonderful gifts they are! What more could a child of God ask? In this prayer, the essence and solemnity of baptism are expressed. Notice that the newly baptized are now called "servants." They have been committed to living a life of service, to living into the kingdom of God, to helping usher in that kingdom in whatever way they can. They are servants because they will learn to care for others and in so doing come to the fullness that God intends for each of them. When we think about what we want for our children, servanthood may not be at the top of our list. We hope they will be responsible, respectful, loving. We want them to be self-assured, successful, hopeful, and faithful. But a servant? Yet this is what baptism is all about. The servant is the one who serves others. Imagine what the world would be like if we all served others, if we all were most concerned with what would help other people get their needs met!

Let's look at these gifts. First, we pray to God to give the newly baptized inquiring and discerning hearts. To inquire means to question, and to discern means to sort through. What a great gift! Just think if our children always asked questions, continued to seek knowledge all their lives. And then having asked the questions, to discern the answers, to sift through all of the information and come to a wise conclusion—and to know this in their hearts. For we pray for inquiring and discerning *hearts*, not minds. We pray they will tune their hearts to God and continually learn how to see and hear and do God's will.

Having these hearts that can know, we then ask for courage: courage to will and to persevere. It's one thing to discern the wise action but quite another to take it. What we hope for the newly baptized is that they'll be able to do those things outlined in the Baptismal Covenant, and when it seems their loving actions are futile, they'll be able to stick with it. As parents and godparents, we want our children to hold on fast to what is good and worthy and loving. We hope they'll persevere in following Christ. And that relates to the third gift: a spirit to know and to love God. To really know someone is to be intimate with them. What would it look like to know God, to be intimate with the Almighty? That is what we pray for—that our children may know and love God. We speak often about God's love for us and our need to love ourselves and others. But do we think much about what it means for us to love God? What does it look like when we love God? We pray that along with those baptismal waters, our children will also be showered with the desire to love God.

In the prayer, we save the best for last: the gift of joy and wonder. Nothing is quite like the joy and wonder of a child. When my children were little, I used to savor each running hug that ended in my arms. I knew they wouldn't show this exuberance forever. Like those running hugs that almost knock you over with their enthusiasm, the joy that children can express so freely is a true gift. We pray here that it will be their gift for life. And we pray that it will be a gift *of* life, a gift that draws them to the created world and entices them to enter into it with the same exuberance. We hope they'll run pell-mell into the arms of God's creation with a great big hug that just might knock God over. We hope they'll look around them with wonder and awe and big eyes with mouths open. This is the church's hope for all people, not just for children. This is the prayer for the newly baptized, regardless of their age. We pray they will have this joy and wonder always!

Welcoming the Newly Baptized

And so the baptismal ritual ends as the congregation, the gathered community, says hello.

"Let us welcome the newly baptized," says the celebrant.

The assembled congregation—parents, godparents, clergy, choir members, acolytes, Sunday school teachers, visitors, ushers, and all present—proclaim, "We receive you into the household of God. Confess the faith of Christ crucified, proclaim his resurrection, and share with us in his eternal priesthood." Like the receiving blanket that swaddles a newborn, the congregation gathers the newly baptized into its midst and wraps her or him in a loving embrace of pride, welcome, and expectation. The congregation acts like the enthusiastic host, welcoming a long-expected and hoped-for guest into a home. Yet the congregation offers even more than welcome. "We receive you," the people say. We welcome friends and strangers; we receive a gift.

To receive the newly baptized is to acknowledge the gift of this person for the community. It suggests that we have been waiting for them, that their place in the household of God has been there all along, ready and waiting for them to enter into it. The newly baptized take up a permanent place in their new home, the body of Christ, the household of God. The people already there are excited about it. It's a joyous occasion. There's so much to look forward to in this new place, this new home. From this moment on, the newly baptized, even those only a month old, take on full membership in this body. From this moment, they are to confess the faith, proclaim the good news, and share in the ministry of the people of God. As The Book of Common Prayer states, baptism is full initiation. There is no other test to pass, no other ritual to perform. This is it. The game is on. The life in Christ blossoms!

So you have done it. You have completed the baptismal ritual with your child. You have made the promises and been prayed over. Now what?

Getting Your Feet Wet

Things to Think About

- What is your greatest hope for your child in and through baptism?
- What baptismal gifts did your child receive? From family and friends? From the church? From you?
- How do you embody your love for God? How do you live out the call to servanthood? What might your child learn from your witness and example?
- How can you as a parent (or godparent) help the body of Christ keep the promises it has made to your child in the baptismal service?

Things to Do

- Plan to celebrate your child's baptismal anniversary. Light the baptismal candle, say a special prayer, and tell the story of your child's baptismal day. Encourage godparents to send cards or call on that day.
- Make a commitment to attend worship regularly with your child. Infants and adults alike can soak up the atmosphere of a loving and supportive community. Even a church nursery is a place where your child can experience the care and nurture that are part of the body of Christ.

PART 2
Family Ritual and Practice

When I was in my late twenties, I was asked to write a spiritual autobiography. I had joined a small group at my church, and each member was asked to think about how God had been present throughout his or her life. It was in doing this that I realized how much my faith had been formed within two loving communities: the Episcopal Church and my family. Since that time I've prepared many such autobiographies, and in the process of writing each one, I've discovered more and more how God has been at work in my life. When I presented that first spiritual autobiography to that small group, I said that my family didn't just attend church—we lived in faith. Twenty years later, I still believe this is an accurate description of my childhood home. One of the reasons I am passionate about faith formation in the home is because my childhood home was a faithful community that formed me as a Christian. Communities have much to teach us, and we'll learn many things if we stay the course through all the ups and downs. The family, or household, is one such community. For good or bad, we are formed by the communities in which we live, the households in which we reside. My parents were wonderful about household ritual, daily prayer, and celebration of faith traditions.

Let me be quick to point out that neither my family nor the Episcopal Church I grew up in was perfect. As with most experiences, there's more than one story to tell about my childhood, for I had both joyful and painful times. But the story I tell here is about how I was introduced to a rich faith experience that spoke to me of God's love at an early age and sustained me during wilderness times of personal and communal woe and tragedy. As my husband and children and I continue to explore the expanding territory that is our household, we're not exempt from missteps, loss, and real pain. I don't begin to think that my husband and I parent perfectly, but I do believe we parent faithfully—we stick with the task, learn along the way, confess our failings, offer and look for forgiveness, and encounter the abundant love of God.

One of my favorite stories that Jesus tells is about the wise man and the foolish man.

> "Everyone then who hears these words of mine and acts on them will be like a wise man who built his house on rock. The rain fell, the floods came, and the winds blew and beat on that house, but it did not fall, because it had been founded on rock. And everyone who hears these words of mine and does not act on them will be like a foolish man who built his house on sand. The rain fell, and the floods came, and the winds blew and beat against that house, and it fell—and great was its fall!" (Matthew 7:24–27)

What I find important to remember about this story is that the rains and the floods came to both houses. The wise man did not escape disaster. Rather, after the disaster, his house was still standing. The firm foundation helped the house remain intact and be able to continue after the storm. There's no way to parent that I know about that will prevent disaster. But I believe that if we pay attention to the foundation on which our households are built, we can withstand a good amount of rain. The task of parenting is daunting when you really get your mind around it. But it's a task I approach with real joy. My hope is that the stories, experiences, and approaches offered in this book are helpful to other parents and godparents.

Part 2 of this book looks at practical ways to celebrate faith in the home. It takes the five promises found at the end of the Baptismal Covenant (see pages 46–47) and turns them toward the household. In the church we often use these five promises to talk about how we can enact our faith in the world. This is most appropriate. We're called as Christians to respond to the world around us with love, justice, and mercy. Our Baptismal Covenant gives us a framework for ethical action. Yet our households are also arenas in which we can choose to behave ethically. In fact, the more we practice the promises of the Baptismal Covenant within our households, the better we'll be able to live out in the world the commitments of a baptized life.

In describing an ethic of behavior, Jesus takes the 613 commandments contained in Jewish Scripture and distills them into what we call the two great commandments.

One of the scribes came near and heard them disputing with one another, and seeing that he answered them well, he asked him, "Which commandment is the first of all?" Jesus answered, "The first is, 'Hear, O Israel: the Lord our God, the Lord is one; you shall love the Lord your God with all your heart, and with all your soul, and with all your mind, and with all your strength.' The second is this, 'You shall love your neighbor as yourself.' There is no other commandment greater than these." (Mark 12:28–31)

The first commandment is the one that Moses taught the people of Israel thousands of years earlier (Deuteronomy 6:4–5). It is called the *Shema* in Jewish tradition and is one of the most important prayers of a faithful person. The second commandment Jesus chooses comes from the book of Leviticus (19:18). Christians call these two commandments the summary of the law. Its two parts—love of God and love of neighbor—hold in dynamic tension all that we are called to as Christian people. Likewise, this is our calling as parents and godparents.

In Luke's Gospel, the teaching of the summary of the law is followed by this question: "Who is my neighbor?" The parable of the Good Samaritan is told in response (Luke 10:29–37). The answer to this question may seem obvious to us, especially as the Good Samaritan story along with the commandment to love your neighbor as yourself are fairly well known in our culture. Yet often the most familiar teachings of Jesus bear much fruit if we spend some time getting beyond what we think we know about them. Father, teacher, and priest Thomas Breidenthal takes a close look behind this commandment in his book *Christian Households: The Sanctification of Nearness*. Breidenthal reminds us that "the word 'neighbor' means someone who is *nigh* to me, near to me."[7] Who is nearer to us on a daily basis than the people we share a home with?

It's helpful to identify the people who share a home as a "household" rather than using the term "family" exclusively. Both are appropriate terms. But the word "family" can bring to mind all-too-familiar stereotypes of what a family should look like. In practice, families come in all shapes and sizes and may consist of a variety of combinations of adults and children; they may be intergenerational, blended, or transitional; children may be biological, adopted, or fostered. A household is a specific community in which, by definition, its members are neighbors; they are, after all, near to one another. For many people the household is the primary community in which faith is formed. Even if you belong to and are active in a church or other faith community, those aren't the people you share meals and bathrooms with every day. It's in the home that you constantly bump up against those nigh to you. It's in the household that you have the most opportunities to form and practice your faith. So what would it look like to "respect the dignity of every human being" in your own household? How do we live out the Baptismal Covenant in our homes?

The next chapters give some thought to the answers to these questions. In them you will find many parenting stories, guidelines, and tips about faith formation for day-to-day life in the home. Again, the "Getting Your Feet Wet" sections at the end of each chapter suggest things to think about and things to do. Keep in mind that parenting is always a work in progress. If you are new to parenting or just beginning to tackle faith formation in your home for the first time, choose one or two ideas to try. Find the issues or practices that you are most drawn to and have the most energy for. Following our passions is often a way to discover our gifts. When you bring your own gifts and passions to parenting, you will be nurturing yourself as well as your household. Remember that you too are a child of God and on your own spiritual path.

CHAPTER SEVEN

Play and Pray

*"Will you continue in the Apostles' teaching
and fellowship, in the breaking of bread
and in the prayers?"*

The apostles were some of the first Christians. The Greek word "apostle" was a technical term in the time of Jesus, a job description. An apostle was someone who was sent on a mission to proclaim a message. The followers of Jesus who became apostles not only delivered their messages, but lived those messages.

Apostles aren't exactly the same as disciples. A disciple is a follower of a particular person or teaching. Jesus had many disciples, including women and men of many different social classes. Of those, there were "the Twelve" and later "the Seventy," who were set aside for specific ministry. None of them were initially apostles of the full gospel message. The first apostle could be said to be Mary Magdalene. On Easter Day, Mary was the first to witness the risen Christ, and she was sent to tell the others. This is why she is called the apostle to the apostles. Other followers of Jesus became apostles. Some, like Peter, were among the Twelve. Others, like Paul, had never been disciples during Jesus' lifetime. Their writings make up the New Testament. So whenever we read and study the Bible, we are encountering the teaching of the apostles. And there is more. There are other writings. There are creeds and early church documents that witness to what the apostles did and taught.

So as the first Christians, the first who believed that Jesus was the Christ, the messiah of God, the apostles began to live lives based on their relationship with Christ and to invite others into their community. The beginning of their ministry is told in the story of Pentecost. Jesus had promised them that they would be baptized by the Holy Spirit. Sure enough, about fifty days after the resurrection, the apostles were hanging out together when suddenly a violent wind rushed through the room, flames appeared on their heads, and they were filled with the Holy Spirit. Hearing the commotion, a crowd gathered; the apostles' immediate response was to begin teaching. As the people around them wondered about this presence of the Holy Spirit, Peter told the crowd about Jesus and what the scriptures said about him—that Jesus is truly the messiah. The people who heard him were stunned—they were "cut to the heart"—and asked what they should do. Repent and be baptized was the answer. And so they were, and scripture tells us that about three thousand people became converts that day. And what happened next? How did they live into their baptisms? "They devoted themselves to the apostles' teaching and fellowship, to the breaking of bread and the prayers" (Acts 2:42). So there it is. This first promise of the Baptismal Covenant comes straight from scripture. It is what the earliest Christians did.

Teaching

How do you as parents and godparents continue in the apostles' teaching? It helps to remember that none of the apostles were seminary educated or ordained. They were women and men who had their hearts changed by Christ and went on to tell about it. Some of them, like Paul, were quite educated and sophisticated. Some of them, like Lydia, were businesswomen. Some of them, like Mary Magdalene, came from wealth. Some of them, like Peter, were day laborers. Some of them, like Mary the mother of Jesus, had raised children. The point is, you don't need to be theologically educated to share your love of Christ with your children. I think to continue in the apostles' teaching means two things. It means to share with our children what the apostles knew, and it means to share with them what we know. One of the easiest ways to share what the apostles knew is to read what's in the Bible.

When I was twelve, a friend and I decided we were going to read the entire Bible from beginning to end. So we sat down and began with Genesis, thinking that surely the way to read the Bible was the same way we read a storybook, from start to finish. We got lost early on in the lists of "begats." The Bible, we discovered, isn't one storybook that you can read from start to finish, but a collection of sacred writings that tell the great story of God's love for God's people. It certainly contains stories. It also contains poetry and history and letters and lists of genealogies. So when you want to share the Bible, our sacred writings, with your children, a good way to begin is to read them Bible stories.

There are many ways to share Bible stories with your children. Beautifully illustrated Bible-story books for children, as well as videos and DVDs, are a great place to start. A list of some of my favorites is found in the resources section at the back of this book. Singing Bible songs is another great way for children to learn stories. When my children were young, we often listened to Bible songs when we were in the car. We especially loved the ones that told stories, such as "Zaccheus Was a Wee Little Man" (Luke 19:1–10) and "The Wise Man Built His House upon the Rock" (Matthew 7:24–27). There are also many wonderful stories that don't come from the Bible directly but teach about love, respect, creation, and other important topics. The teaching of the apostles is found in our tradition and stories of the early church as well as in the Bible. Illustrated lives of the saints or the creeds or prayers also pass along the teaching of the apostles from one generation to another. And when children become readers, their own children's Bible will help them look up the stories themselves and see where they come from.

It's not really necessary to set aside specific time for Bible reading. In our household, we read together most evenings. We let the girls choose a story each night as part of our bedtime routine. Our house is full of children's books, including beautiful Bible stories and tales of saints, so these are among the ones they choose. I enjoy setting out different books for different seasons. During Advent I pull out the Christmas storybooks, and during Lent the Easter ones are put on display in the house. Thus, the stories of our faith tradition are interwoven with classics of children's literature into a rich fabric of story, history, poetry, adventure, and life.

Fellowship

For teaching to be helpful and effective, it needs to take place within a community. Faithful people are formed, not educated into being. If the household is to be a community in which the content of the faith tradition can be taught, then it must be a community of intentional fellowship. What is fellowship? Well, in simplest terms it means spending time together. The early apostles were very intentional about how they spent time together. In fact, they first lived in one community sharing all of their resources in common. They spent time together in the temple and shared meals in each other's homes. The fellowship they shared was larger than one household, but it was one in which they called each other sister and brother. They gathered for meals, instruction, work, and decision making.

It may seem obvious, but it's important for us to spend time with the people in our family, especially those in our household. Just living together under one roof doesn't guarantee fellowship. What with workloads and commuting hours and scheduling of children's activities, it's easy for a family to lose sight of fellowship altogether, and it's possible to live together without taking the time or effort to connect with one another. Household fellowship has to be intentional. It does take time and effort. Yet fellowship can happen in many different ways—around the breakfast table, during a family outing, or in planning a family vacation.

One helpful vehicle for encouraging fellowship is the family meeting, a designated time when the entire household gathers to take care of business. Not only do such meetings help the business of family life move more smoothly, but they also provide bonding time. On the advice of a friend and parenting teacher, my husband and I started family meetings before we had children. They helped us to be respectful of each other as we went about our busy lives and careers. They guaranteed that once a week we spent intentional time together to honor each other as well as work together to keep the household business afloat. Once we had children, and as our children grew, we adapted our family meeting. We added elements that each member could participate in, no matter their age. And we incorporated suggestions from the girls so that the form of the meeting was something everyone agreed to. We found that it was important for this time to include play and prayer as well as business.

Currently our family meeting begins with a song that someone chooses. Next we each tell something important—good or bad—that happened to us that day. Then we share compliments. Each family member compliments each other member—and we have to compliment ourselves as well. This exercise helps us to take note of each person in the family. Then we bring up any concerns. Can we get a new pet? Who will take the car in to get the oil changed? Where do we want to go on vacation? We go over the schedule for the week so we remember all of the meetings, classes, and special pick-up times. Finally we hand out allowances and end with prayer. Everyone comes to the family meeting and everyone participates. It makes a huge difference in helping our week run smoothly. It also molds who we are as a family. As we give and share compliments, listen to one another's concerns, and solve problems as a family, we build our family identity and shape our values. The meetings, like our family, are a work in progress. Both are work well worth doing.

In addition to family meeting time, it's vitally important for the entire household to gather regularly for play. There are so many ways to do this: playing a board game together, singing around the piano, watching a movie, doing a jigsaw puzzle, playing catch, or going for a walk. It's also important for household members to spend one-on-one time with each other. As a wife, it's important for me to have time with my husband that is just about our relationship and the fun we can have. As a mother, it's important for me to spend separate time with each of my daughters. As a father, it's important for my husband to do the same. And the girls enjoy their sister time as well. These times of bonding between individuals help the bonding of the whole. After all, how can you be in a relationship with someone if you never spend any time with them?

Breaking of Bread

A few years back, my husband and I both took new jobs and moved to another state so that we could have dinner together as a family. That's how important table fellowship is in our life together. Before the move, my husband's work hours and commute made it impossible for him to be home in time for dinner much of the time. After our first child was born, this problem became intolerable. We both wanted that time together. After little success trying to shorten the commute by finding a new place to live, we decided to start over. Once we opened ourselves up to the possibility of rearranging our lives, all sorts of opportunities presented themselves. We both looked for new jobs. We found them within two weeks of each other in the same town—in a new state. It certainly seemed that God was calling us to this new place. So we moved. In our new community, neither of us has to drive more than twenty minutes to get to work, and eight years and another child later, family dinner remains the most important event in our day.

How do we break bread in a household? We do it every time we eat. In church this breaking of the bread refers to communion or Holy Eucharist. In the home, it refers to the dining room table, which can also be holy. We all have to eat. Parents need to provide healthy food for their children. Making an effort to have meals together on a regular basis is good for the entire household. It is breaking bread together. Regularly sharing meals provides connection, stability, and nurture. When sitting down at the table, members of the household can talk to one another, check in on each other's day, and reconnect after time apart. When this connection happens often, it provides stability. Each member of the household expects it to happen and can count on it. It improves the household rhythm. Time spent in the company of one another also nurtures each of the relationships in the household. Eating together is one of the basic ways we experience community and celebrate. So the more we share this activity on a daily basis with those we love, the more we will bond together.

It's not always easy to find this time. One family I know gathers on Friday evenings in their pajamas for a pizza party and movie night. This weekly gathering helps nurture their strong family bond. Another family sometimes packs a picnic dinner and meets at the father's workplace when he has evening duty. Meal sharing doesn't always have to be in the house. A nice meal out is also wonderful, especially if it's in a place the entire family enjoys.

For mealtime to be life giving to the family, it needs to include everyone in the household. One parenting book my husband and I read said that three-year-olds couldn't manage table manners and it was better to feed them in the kitchen before the adults sat down at the table. We couldn't do that. Eating dinner together as a family is one of our core values. It's true that three-year-olds struggle with table manners, but we chose to struggle together. For a while, mealtime wasn't always pleasant for the adults. Sometimes it was (and still can be) the occasion for meltdowns. But we parent at the dining room table as well as other places. And our kids know the value of our dinner table. We light a candle, we say grace, we eat. We excuse the kids when they have finished eating and my husband and I linger at the table for some adult time. We all miss it when it doesn't happen.

Prayer

My younger daughter and I like to color our prayers together. Next to her room is a small room we call our "prayer room." It has just enough space for a chair, a desk, and a small bookshelf. We all use it as a quiet space. In it we keep objects that remind us of the holy: prayer beads, an icon, a fall leaf, collected stones, and a sketchbook. I often go there in the morning before the rest of the household is awake. I sit in the comfortable chair and am quiet. Sometimes I pray out of the prayer book, sometimes I read, sometimes I am contemplative. In this quiet, I can hear my daughter awake in the next room. I feel as well as hear her young body stretch, I hear her feet touch the floor, and I'm filled with delight at the sound of her footsteps padding across the floor. When she comes out of her room, she often senses my quiet presence and enters the prayer room. The coloring began when I suggested it as a way to keep her in the room with me while I finished some reading I needed to do for the day. I enjoyed her company and didn't want her to leave. So she took out the pastels and the sketchbook and began. It has become her morning prayer. Sometimes we color together. Sometimes her sister joins us. I've begun to see that sketchbook as a prayer journal.

Prayer invites us into God's presence. Since we live within God's creation, we're always in God's presence, yet we often go about our days unconscious of this truth. Prayer is the language that nurtures our relationship with God as God's beloved children. The possibilities for prayer are endless. Sometimes we pray alone, and sometimes we pray with others. Sometimes we use set words, and sometimes we make it up as we go along. Sometimes we pray out loud, and sometimes we pray silently. We can sing our prayers or dance our prayers or draw our prayers. Sometimes we pray in serenity, and sometimes we pray in panic. Someone once told me that perhaps the two truest prayers are "Help me, help me, help me!" and "Thank you, thank you, thank you!" Prayer in your household doesn't have to be rigid or complicated. All household members can be included, regardless of age.

One of our favorite family graces is one that our older daughter composed when she was three; it goes, "Thanks for this food and blessings flow. Amen."[8] We love how she combined elements of prayers she had heard into her own delightful song. Our younger daughter composed another prayer we use: "God be with us day and night, in the Spirit and in the Light. Amen."[9] This began as one of her bedtime prayers and makes use of her enjoyment of rhyme. Each of the girls' prayers is unique, bursting with the author's personality. Our use of them in our home makes them part of our family album.

One of my favorite descriptions of prayer is in Douglas Wood's *Grandad's Prayers of the Earth*, beautifully illustrated by P. J. Lynch. In it, a grandfather tells his grandson, "Most prayers are not really questions. . . . And if we listen closely, a prayer is often its own answer. Like the trees and winds and waters, we pray because we are here—not to change the world, but to change ourselves."[10]

There are all sorts of opportunities for prayer in the household. One of the simplest ways to add prayer to your day is to look for existing transitions and routines that lend themselves to a prayerful thought. When the family sits down to meals, begin with a simple grace. If you have a household routine of putting the children to bed, include a prayer. If you enjoy waking your children in the morning, instead of saying, "Rise and shine," why not greet them with a Scripture passage such as, "Arise, shine; for your light has come" (Isaiah 60:1 or Canticle 11 in the BCP)? There are many places to find prayers for these occasions, including The Book of Common Prayer and collections of family prayers or prayers for children (see the resources section at the back of this book).

Important events in family life and the seasons of the church year are also wonderful occasions for prayer. You can pray for family members on their birthdays or baptismal anniversaries or before they leave for travel or as they graduate from school. You can have a house blessing for a new home. You can say a special prayer when you light an Advent wreath or put up a Christmas tree or gather for Easter dinner.

You can pray in times of crisis or rejoicing. You can pray with family members who are ill or for a beloved animal companion who has died. You can pray with a child who has a scary dream in the night or for a spouse who has a rough day of work ahead. You can pray in thanksgiving for the arrival of a much-anticipated visitor or to welcome a new member of the household. You can include prayer in family celebrations of a new job, a wonderful performance, or a significant accomplishment by a household member. One family I met used to keep the Christmas cards they received in the dining room; as the new year began, they would select a card at dinnertime and give thanks for the people who had sent it to them.

Teaching, fellowship, the breaking of bread, and prayer will look different in each household. With practice, you'll discover what works for you. It doesn't need to be obvious or overstated to be significant—it's more important that these things be a part of the fabric of your day and the rhythm of your household than that they follow a prescribed method or pattern. Applying these practices is about nurturing your faith, not about hitting you over the head with "religion." When well knit into the fabric of the household, these practices are embraced and adapted by all household members so that they bring joy and comfort, a sense of stability and even playfulness.

Getting Your Feet Wet

Things to Think About

- What was your experience of the Bible when you were growing up? What would you hope for your child in terms of familiarity with the Bible by the time he or she is a young adult?
- How do you play together as a household?
- When do you share mealtimes as a household? What occasions do you celebrate with food?
- How do you pray? With words? Images? In quiet? Are you comfortable praying with members of your family? How might you increase your comfort?

Things to Do

- Read Bible stories with your children out of a children's Bible or family Bible. For even more fun, try acting one out.
- Set a regular time for a weekly family gathering to foster bonding among household members.
- Make meal time sacred time. Gather the household, set an inviting table, light candles, and say grace. Invite children to contribute by making up their own prayers or creating seasonal centerpieces.
- Add prayer to your existing routine. Try bedtime prayers, grace at meals, prayers to mark special occasions, or blessings on children before they leave for school.

CHAPTER EIGHT

We All Make Mistakes

"Will you persevere in resisting evil, and, whenever you fall into sin, repent and return to the Lord?"

A friend and colleague of mine came home from work one day to find his household—his wife, one hyperactive four-year-old, two two-year-olds who were being potty trained, and a young puppy who was being housebroken—in a state of chaos and confusion. He discovered the children huddled in their rooms, the dog curled up in a corner, and his wife collapsed in a puddle of guilt on the sofa. It had been a bad day. For the umpteenth time—just one too many—someone had had an "accident." As my friend surveyed the devastating scene, he was hit with a wave of guilt as he realized he'd been too absent for far too long. That repentance and forgiveness were needed was obvious. But how to achieve them was beyond comprehension.

We've all been there. So it's actually comforting that this baptismal promise says, "Whenever you fall into sin," not "If you fall into sin." The statement assumes that we'll make mistakes. It's inevitable that we'll fall short of the mark when it comes to treating those in our household with love and respect. This doesn't mean we're bad people to begin with. In fact, scripture tells us we're good. All that God created is good. God said so. "God saw everything that he had made, and indeed, it was very good" (Genesis 1:31).

The "whenever" refers to our limited human nature. We're not perfect—and all attempts to be perfect will fail. But when we fail as Christians, we can do something about it. We can admit we are lost, turn to God, and ask for help. This is called repenting, or being sorry. The word "repent" means to turn. What this promise models for us is that when we fail—either a little bit or utterly—we can turn back to God. In fact, the promise includes the phrase

73

"return to the Lord." You can only return to a place you've been before. We have a home in God's presence to which we can return whenever we stray.

The point is, it's just not possible to parent perfectly. No matter how many parenting classes you take or how many parenting books you read, you're still a vulnerable, limited human being. Frankly, I find it a great relief to acknowledge that I don't parent perfectly. I remember once when I confessed to a friend that after yelling at my then three-year-old daughter over some now-forgotten incident, I went into the laundry room, collapsed on the floor, and sobbed because I was such a horrible mother. My friend was relieved. Not because I'd chosen to confide in her, but because she thought she was the only one who ever lost her temper at her child and then felt like a failure. After that conversation, we learned to share our parenting trials with each other often. We had gifts to offer one another—the gift of understanding, of accepting each other as worthy mothers even with all our faults, of reminding each other that we were loved and could be forgiven.

We might as well be honest about the fact that there will be times when we'll hurt others in our household. What really matters is not that we lose it with our spouse or partner or children, but what we do next. This promise points toward two tasks. One is being truly sorry and repenting of our hurtful actions. The other is working toward better relationships with all in our household.

To repent means to acknowledge our fault and to want to make it right. As parents, we teach our children to say "I'm sorry." Yet we all know times when saying sorry and being sorry are not the same thing. True repentance means not only to acknowledge a wrong we've done, but to feel sad about it and want to make it right. Once we have done this, the next step is to return to the Lord. We seek God's forgiveness for our shortcomings. The good news is that God always forgives us. God offers this gift to us, and we have only to open our hearts and hands to receive it. Forgiveness is not always an easy gift to receive. It seems to me we're far more likely to avoid it altogether by pretending either that we don't need forgiveness or that we haven't really done anything so wrong. Sometimes we refuse to believe that we are worthy of forgiveness, and we hold on to our guilt as proof that we are, in fact, despicable people who cannot be forgiven for our bad deeds. Even so, God's forgiveness stands. We can't earn it or work for it. It's simply showered upon us. After all, when we say in the earlier part of the Baptismal Covenant that we believe in "the forgiveness of sins," we really mean that forgiveness is available to us. So when we fail, we turn around again, face God, and go on living.

Repenting Is Hard Work

Our younger daughter had a complete meltdown one morning. Of course it happened as we were just about to leave the house. I was leaving to walk our older daughter to school and then head directly for work, and my husband was about to put our younger daughter in the car and drop her off at pre-school on his way to work. She didn't want to go. She cried and said she hated school (normally she loved her school). We told her she had no choice. Her attitude didn't improve. Time was of the essence. She stubbornly refused to cooperate. My husband and I tried tag-team parenting without success. Tempers flared on all sides.

Finally I decided to pull rank. I picked her up, carried her screaming, writhing body out to the car, and buckled her into her car seat. She continued to scream as she unbuckled herself. We were defeated. There was no way my husband could drive safely without her calm and buckled. At this point I gave up. I left to walk our other daughter to school, feeling like a failure as a parent and a spouse. My husband, already late for work, returned to the house with our sobbing daughter. He was angry and let her know how upset he was. She finally flung herself into his arms, barely able to speak the words "I'm sorry." He held her close and said, "I'm sorry too." They each took several deep breaths and eventually calmed down.

There was a need for a lot of repentance in our house that day. We were all hit by the emotional shrapnel. I felt bad that I had allowed the argument to escalate and guilty that I had tried to force my daughter into her car seat. I felt I had failed my husband by leaving him alone to solve the problem. My husband felt bad that he had lost his temper with his younger daughter. Our older daughter felt sad for her sister and unhappy that our family was in an uproar. And our younger daughter felt overwhelmed by a complex mix of emotions and was remorseful about her actions. Sometimes forgiveness is quite complicated. Our conflicts don't easily fall into categories of who's wrong and who's right. Forgiveness is not just about one person offering it while another one receives it. Active repentance requires us to be open to giving and receiving forgiveness at the same time. To do this, we must be willing to accept our own limitations as parents as well as the limitations of our children.

Opportunity for Improvement

In this promise we also agree to "persevere in resisting evil." At the same time that we acknowledge our human limitations, we're also called to strive to become more and more the people God would have us be. Our scriptures, the teachings of the church, and the life of Jesus all call us to be compassionate and kind, to treat one another well—and we all fall short. When we recognize our faults, we also need to make an effort to change any habits we have that hurt others.

A parishioner once told me he was practicing a spiritual discipline whereby for one week he would not have to say "I'm sorry" to anyone in his family. "A week?" I exclaimed. "I couldn't make it through a single day without having to apologize to someone in my household!" I think the point of the exercise was to help him become more aware of some of his actions that might be hurtful to his family and then not do them. But the trap I saw was the belief that it is somehow possible to "be good," that we're capable of choosing only right actions. I've never found it a successful plan to just get up one morning and will to be good. It never works. Sheer will simply isn't enough. As the apostle Paul says, "I can will what is right, but I cannot do it. For I do not do the good I want, but the evil I do not want is what I do" (Romans 7:18–19). We are all limited human beings. It is impossible for us to treat each other perfectly. If we could, we would have no need of the salvation offered by Jesus Christ. Somehow our daily life in Christ is one in which we strive to make good choices while acknowledging our faults and our need for forgiveness. The rhythm of our life is one of repentance and return.

Forgiveness in the Home

I'm not sure how the argument started. My daughters were doing something when suddenly a fight erupted. One came running, asking me to intervene.

My first foray into the melee seemed like an ordinary untangling of an argument. Then my older daughter, in a fit of anger, stomped her foot, screwed up her face, put it within an inch of her sister's, and threatened her. I am the youngest child in my family. With two older brothers, I am quite familiar with the feeling of being threatened by an angry older sibling. So watching my two daughters at that moment, I lost it. I stomped my foot at the older one, screwed up my face, put it within an inch of hers, and yelled, "Don't threaten your sister!" So much for patient parenting.

It's so easy for our children to step on our most vulnerable spots. Whatever wounds you experienced as a child are sure to come to the surface as you parent. There is a certain truth in the Hebrew proverb, "The parents have eaten sour grapes, and the children's teeth are set on edge" (Jeremiah 31:29; Ezekiel 18:2). On one hand, this proverb can be used as an excuse: "Our parents messed up, and now we have to pay the price." On the other hand, it can be used to shed light on our own actions: "I was hurt as a child, and I am now living out that hurt in my parenting." If we recognize the childhood hurts that still haunt us as adults, we can begin to modify our behavior. We don't have to perpetuate certain attitudes and behaviors. We can make different choices. Rather than seeing this as a vicious circle, we can do something to change the cycle. We can see a situation like this as a wonderful opportunity to experience repentance and forgiveness.

Many adults I talk to say they have no memory of their parents apologizing to them. It's easy for us as adults to think we'll lose something if we apologize to our children. After all, we are the adults, the ones in power. But how do we expect our children to learn about repentance and forgiveness if we don't model it for them? How can we expect them to say they're sorry if we don't?

After that horrible moment with my daughter, and after we'd both spent some time in tears, I went to her and apologized. "I'm sorry I yelled at you," I said. "I was feeling angry, but it was wrong of me to yell at you like that. I love you very much, and I don't want to hurt you." I left it there. For us to be reconciled at that moment, she just needed to hear that I was sorry I had hurt her. For us to be reconciled, I needed to apologize without any strings attached.

I don't think I gave away my responsibility as the parent in that moment. I wish I hadn't lost my temper. But since I had, I needed to make it right with her and with God. I had fallen into sin. I needed God's forgiveness as well as hers. This is an action that is often beyond us. What do we do when we have done the unforgivable? That's when we most need to remember that we rely on God. We need to remember, as a colleague of mine says, that "forgiveness is not an act of will; it is a function of divine grace."[11] It's helpful to remember once again that when we make these baptismal promises, we do so "with God's help."

So with God's help, we persevere in resisting evil; we work to change habits that hurt. With God's help we repent when we fall into sin; we say we are sorry to any member of our household whom we have hurt. With God's help we return to the Lord; we open our hearts to receive God's love and forgiveness.

Giving Enough Room

A friend of mine talks about the moment he discovered that giving his daughter a time-out was much more effective than a literal slap on the wrist. He describes one of the truly sad moments in his life as the day when his four-year-old daughter said something that made him so angry he smacked her little leg with his hand. As he began to tell her why he had punished her, she told him she hadn't said what he thought he had heard. He listened. He apologized. He told her he would never hit her again. And he never did. It turns out his father used to strike like that, and my friend had always told himself he'd never do that to his children. That incident taught him the value of a time-out.

Many parents have learned that "time out" is effective not only for their children but for themselves as well. I'm often the one who needs time out in tense situations to clear my head and choose the actions I want to make—rather than reacting to a situation I may not completely understand or one that tempts me to act out of some need of my own. What my friend learned from his experience that day was that two images of himself were at play: the shadow of a punishing father and the love he knows in God. The shadow of his father had taken the foreground, but with time for pause, his knowledge of God's love for him washed that shadow away. He says that moment changed him far more than ever it changed his daughter. It helped to heal a wound.

Forgiveness is a life-changing act—both when we seek it out and when we enact it. In the Lord's Prayer, we pray, "Forgive us our trespasses as we forgive those who trespass against us." To trespass is to step out of line, to cross a boundary, to enter forbidden territory. In the context of moral behavior, it means to violate an ethical code of conduct. It means to sin. As parents, we need to ask our children's forgiveness when we have trespassed, when we have stepped over the boundary of loving behavior. And we also need to forgive them their trespasses. Not seeking forgiveness and withholding forgiveness are both harmful to us. Writer Anne Lamott says that choosing not to forgive is like drinking rat poison and expecting the rat to die. In her own struggle to forgive a woman, she writes, "I prayed about it. I prayed because my son loves her son, and my son is so kind that it makes me want to be a better person. . . . I prayed for a miracle; I wrote her name down on a piece of paper, folded it up, and put it in the box that I use as God's In box. 'Help,' I said to God."[12]

That's a good model for enacting forgiveness in the home. When we recognize the need for forgiveness, we can pray about it. That prayer can be a simple offering up of our need to God. As one of my friends is fond of saying, we don't need to give God instructions when we pray; God has a pretty good idea of what needs doing. After months of struggle, Anne Lamott realized one day that she was no longer holding a grudge against this woman. What she discovered—what many people discover—is that forgiveness often comes quietly, unexpectedly, lovingly.

Confession and the Church

The church also teaches us the importance of being sorry. In church we call this confession. Our churches offer many opportunities for confession. We say a corporate confession during Sunday morning worship. Forms of confession are also found in the services of Morning Prayer, Evening Prayer, and Compline in The Book of Common Prayer. On Ash Wednesday the church offers special worship services to begin the season of Lent with a commitment to repentance, or penitence. In the Lord's Prayer, which we say often, we ask for forgiveness and promise to practice forgiveness. All of these provide an opportunity to practice and talk about the importance of forgiveness with the members of our household.

Getting Your Feet Wet

Things to Think About

- What is the biggest mistake you fear making in raising your child in a life of faith? What do you imagine God's response would be to this mistake?
- How would you respond to the declaration, "Forgiveness is the key to healthy relationships"?
- Where do you believe you need to persevere in your parenting? What unhelpful habits or behaviors do you wish to change? Who or what might help you make this change?
- Which is easier for you, to offer forgiveness or to accept forgiveness?
- How have you experienced God's forgiveness?

Things to Do

- Find some time and space for yourself, and think of the things for which you wish to be forgiven. Write a prayer confessing to God your limitations and asking God's forgiveness. Open your heart to God's love.
- Use the following litany during a family prayer time when the need arises or during the penitential season of Lent.

Litany for Forgiveness

For harsh words spoken
We're sorry, God.

For silence that wounds
We're sorry, God.

For hands that hit
We're sorry, God.

For ears that close
We're sorry, God.

For gifts not shared
We're sorry, God.

For [include your own words here]
We're sorry, God.

For hearts not open
We're sorry, God.

Create in us a clean heart, O God.
And renew a right spirit within us.[13]

CHAPTER NINE

Parenting Loud and Clear

*"Will you proclaim by word and example
the Good News of God in Christ?"*

One fall I took my two daughters to a store to buy lunch boxes and back-packs for school. They ran ahead of me to the wall displaying many enticing choices. Two young women were nearby, shopping for items for their college dorm room. They delighted in seeing my young girls choosing backpacks and started to make suggestions. But some of the bags they suggested were adorned with cartoon characters or symbols that were out of bounds for my girls. My husband and I had been clear about which cartoon characters imparted values that we thought fit our family, and we weren't shy about telling our girls why we made those choices. In many cases, we simply weren't happy that products and characters that were fine for teenagers were marketed to six-year-olds. I was delightfully surprised and pleased to hear my girls say, "Oh no, we're not allowed to choose that one." They had gotten the message. They had heard and understood the limits we had given them and were willing to accept them. Without complaint, they chose backpacks that fit our guidelines. And they had fun doing so.

I didn't need my kids to proclaim the gospel according to advertising or popular culture icons. In our family, we've made a decision to proclaim something else.

Proclamation Made Easy

When we see or hear the word "proclaim," we usually think of speaking out. That in turn leads us to visions of preachers on street corners loudly touting their theology. But there are so many ways that we proclaim our beliefs that look nothing like that scene. Proclamation is really about how our actions and words impart our values or our core beliefs. I attended a conference of church educators at which a small group discussed how best to be educators in the church. Much of the energy of our conversation surrounded the difference between formation and education. Most of us saw ourselves engaged in Christian formation rather than Christian education. We agreed that formation is the process of developing a mature faith that begins in infancy and that education about our beliefs and traditions is a component of this formation. We were concerned about process as well as content.

It's much the same with parenting. Faithful parenting is about more than imparting the teachings of Christ. It's also about creating and honoring relationships of integrity with our children, in which we're honest about who we are and what we believe. It's about creating a safe space in which our children can be honest about who they are and what they believe.

Of course there are specific teachings, values, and beliefs we want to pass on to our children. But it's helpful to remember that children grow up and make their own choices about what they believe—they're not robots we can program. But chances are, if we form good relationships with our children, they'll always be open to hearing what we have to say, even if they choose to disagree. If we try to proclaim our faith to our children by sitting them down and telling them what they should believe, we probably won't get very far. But if we live out our faith in what we say and do, our children will experience our proclamation as part of family life. When as parents our words and actions impart to our children the love of God, we are proclaiming the good news. When our words and actions communicate to our children a respect for creation, we are proclaiming the good news. When our words and actions honor the people we encounter on a day-to-day basis, we are proclaiming the good news.

Say What You Mean, Mean What You Say

It helps to be quite clear about what we are communicating. The corporate world—and the world of pop culture—certainly is! Popular musicians, performers, and celebrities express their values blatantly, so as parents we need to be just as clear about ours.

If we say that church is important, for instance, but we seldom attend, then we let our children know that church isn't a big deal to us. Or if we instruct our children to be polite, but we never say please and thank you to them, then we show them that polite behavior isn't important toward the ones closest to us.

Perhaps the most important value we can communicate to our kids is that a life in Christ begins and ends with love. Christian faith holds out the promise that we can live lives that abound with love, hope, forgiveness, respect, justice, and peace. However, as priest and psychologist Paul Donoghue writes, we are inundated "on screen, on stage, on television, in music, with depictions of life that are distorted, that are lies."[14] Whether it's a television program in which a family happily solves a crisis in a twenty-three-minute episode, or a video game in which graphic violence has no negative consequences, or a song playing relentlessly on the radio that subtly but surely reinforces gender stereotypes, we're constantly exposed to views of life that don't align themselves with either our lived experience or the gospel.

We don't have to allow these distortions to be the last word in our homes. We can be honest about the hard work of reconciliation. We can teach about the real grief that inevitably follows violence. We can strive to see our spouses and partners and children for who they are and the gifts they possess and avoid labeling them or stereotyping them. This daily proclamation can happen in simple ways as well as complex ones. When I'm on the road, I have a habit of talking to the drivers of other cars, who are usually blissfully unaware of this one-sided conversation. When a driver slows down to allow me to pull out of the parking lot and into the street, I wave and say thank you out loud. Of course they can't hear me. My older daughter once asked me who I was talking to.

"I'm thanking the driver in that car behind us for letting me make my turn."

"But why, Mommy?"

"Because it's respectful to thank people when they're helpful."

"But they can't hear you."

"I know, but it's still important for me to do it. Even if they can't hear me, I'm still grateful for their help, and I want to acknowledge that."

My words and actions in saying thank you showed that I value recognizing other people for their kindness. The fact that the action was important to me regardless of whether it was received by the intended audience showed that I value expressing gratitude in and of itself. By responding thoughtfully to my daughter's question, I was able to explain the value of politeness to her.

The Teachable Moment

That experience with my daughter is what many educators call a "teachable moment." An opportunity presented itself, and I took advantage of it. If I'd sat my daughter down that morning and said, "Okay, now I'm going to explain to you how to be polite and why being polite is important," she may have taken it in. Maybe. But in this case, she'd experienced on more than one occasion my polite behavior. When she was interested in knowing more about it, she asked. Thus, I was able to proclaim to her, by word and example, what I consider an important value. And she definitely took it in. She may not thank other drivers out loud when she's an adult, but that's not important. What's important to me is that she is polite and treats other people with respect. She's more likely to do this if she sees politeness enacted in our household.

The teachable moment is a great parenting tool. It relieves you of the burden of thinking that you need to lecture your children about your values and allows you to "look for those special times when you can easily bring up issues," as parent educator Debra W. Haffner writes.[15] The more you use this tool, the more opportunities you'll see. Be assured that your children are interested in your values. But in parenting, as in so many things, actions speak louder than words. Your children will absorb the values you enact. So it's a good idea to think about the values you want to pass down to your kids.

Communication Is Key

If we want to clearly communicate our values to our children, we need to be clear about what those values are. It's easier to grasp the teachable moment and run with it if we already know what we want to teach our children. It goes back to the question my husband and I encountered in our first parenting class: What do we want the result of our parenting to be? For one thing, my husband and I want our children to be good stewards of creation. So we try to practice stewardship in the home by recycling newspapers, bottles, and cans, as well as outgrown clothes. We also gratefully receive hand-me-downs and enjoy shopping at the thrift shop. Each trip to the recycling center becomes a lesson in and of itself about taking care of our environment. Because my husband and I are clear about the importance of our care of the earth, it was easy for us to explain why we do these things when our children began to ask.

When new parenting challenges arise, as they inevitably do, my husband and I have to sit down and talk with one another to clarify our values. The girls want to watch a new TV show that we haven't seen. They want to explore a website they heard about at school. They want to buy a toy with their own money. As parents, we take some time before we respond to these requests to think about what we want to communicate. Rather than dealing with each situation as it arises, we try to map out the consequences of our parenting choices. We discuss and decide what criteria we'll use for evaluating TV programs. We set up procedures for safe use of the Internet. We decide how much freedom to give our children in making their own spending choices. Each time we do this, we clarify our values. Then we can more easily communicate those values to our children.

Proclaiming Is a Two-Way Street

One day one of my daughters and I were watching the movie *Ice Age*, in which a sloth, a woolly mammoth, and a saber-toothed tiger bond while trying to return a human infant to his father. At one point, the child, who is learning to walk, pulls hard on the tiger's tail, and when the beast spins around with bared teeth, the child falls on him with a big hug. "Look," said my five-year-old, "the baby is beginning to learn to love. That's good, because if he knows about love, he knows about God." Who would have thought a slapstick comedy could become a vehicle for a child's theological reflection? My daughter had grasped the core of the good news and recognized it when she saw it. She proclaimed it loud and clear, and I delighted in being the recipient of that proclamation.

Our children proclaim to us all the time. Sometimes the teachable moment has us on the learning end of the exchange. A friend tells a story about a moment when her daughter preached the gospel to her. When the tsunami devastated Southeast Asia at the end of 2004, this woman and her family experienced the shock. She and her husband agreed to make what they felt was a sizable donation through an organization linked through his place of work. It never occurred to them that their decision would have a major impact on their thirteen-year-old daughter. She, however, was quite affected. She told her parents that she wanted to make a donation to a group that would help the people suffering the aftereffects of the tsunami.

Together they did some research, and the girl chose a charity. Her parents agreed to write the check on her behalf, and then she could just pay them her saved-up cash. They were stunned, humbled, and deeply moved when she handed them $200—the same amount as the donation they had given. The amount was all their daughter had; it constituted her entire savings, whereas this amount was a fraction of their own earnings.

I am convinced that part of the reason this young woman was able to make such a bold proclamation is that she had witnessed such boldness in her own home. Her parents have been very clear about honoring people in need. From being involved with mission work in their local parish to hosting a Zimbabwean refugee in their small home, their words and actions have shown their daughter how to help people in need. As a family, they believe God will bless their sacrifice. The mother already sees the blessing in her daughter's sacrifice, not only for those she intended to help, but for her family as well. Since she had so little money left after her donation, the young woman took up knitting so she could make, rather than buy, gifts for others.

A Family Identity

My friend's family helps those in need in a hands-on way and is especially concerned with a global sense of ministry. This is part of their family identity. What makes up their identity? All those things that are particular to their household, that bind them together as a cohesive group and define who they are. If this family were to write a family mission statement, it would surely include their desire to reach out to others.

As parents, we try to cast a vision for our household that matches God's vision for us, rather than a distortion of God's vision (like we see all around us). What do we want our children to believe about themselves, life, and life in Christ? Believing in God's love for us and then learning to accept the love of others may be a lifelong learning adventure for all of us. What a great gift we can give our children by taking them along this path with us.

A father had a yearly ritual of taking his daughter ice-skating in New York City during the winter holidays. One of his greatest joys was helping his daughter see the goodness of reaching out to people in need. They had a pact—he'd give her some money to give away to someone who needed it that day. He felt that since they were spending money on themselves for sheer pleasure, they should also do something for others. His daughter's job was to decide who they would help until the money ran out. One night she ordered macaroni and cheese at a restaurant for dinner, but it wasn't like Mom's. She ate only one bite. What should they do with so much food? They agreed they needed to look for someone hungry on the street. They had the waiter wrap it up and found a grateful soul in the subway station.

This was an important ritual for both father and daughter. The father wanted to communicate how much he loved her by spending this important time together. He also wanted her to know something important about God's world. He wanted her to know that we are all connected, our pleasure to another's pleasure or need, even our waste to another's hope. He wanted her to see the goodness in people whom we so often overlook or fear. For him, love is a connection that when acted on makes us real. He and his daughter didn't need to talk about it as much as act it out. This is proclamation. Together, father and daughter proclaimed the good news not only to each other, but also to those with whom they shared their pleasure and good fortune.

Getting Your Feet Wet

Things to Think About

- What kinds of values do you proclaim? Think about a day in the life of your household from the past week. Begin with when you woke up and think through the day. What choices did you make? What values did you impart to your children? Were they values you wanted to impart?
- Who are some parents you admire? What about their parenting would you like to emulate?
- If you could choose a family theme song, what would it be?
- Which of Jesus' teachings are most compelling to you? What core values do they illustrate? Which of these would you like to impart to your children?

Things to Do

- Write a brief mission statement for your household, or make a family banner using important symbols. Be sure to include all household members in the project!
- Talk to your child about the distortions of advertising. Limit the amount of commercial media that your child interacts with each day, such as TV, radio, magazines, and websites. Be aware of commercial appeals that your child encounters on billboards, sides of buses, store signs, Internet pop-ups, and children's products.

CHAPTER TEN

Looking for Love in All the Right Places

"Will you seek and serve Christ in all persons,
loving your neighbor as yourself?"

One day a three-year-old boy in my parish began telling people that he was God. His worried father came to talk to me about it, and I suggested he ask the boy where he'd gotten the idea. The child replied that he had learned it in Sunday school. It seems the children had learned a song based on Psalm 46 featuring the words, "Be still and know that I am God." The boy was somewhat confused about who the "I" was. But he wasn't far off. We are not God, but each of us is created in God's image: "So God created humankind in God's image, in the image of God he created them; male and female he created them" (Genesis 1:27).

We are born holding within us the image of God. Through baptism we are born again so that we may share in the resurrection of Christ. When Christ was raised from the dead, it was a victory over death. Christ's resurrection proved that death was not the last word. God's love reached beyond the sin of the world, beyond the horrible death on the cross, and brought life. God's love continues to reach beyond the sin of the world and touch our very souls. That's why in the baptismal service we pray that "all who are baptized into the death of Jesus Christ . . . may live in the power of his resurrection" and that they may "continue forever in the risen life of Christ" (BCP 306, 307). We're marked by the sign of the cross on our foreheads to signify that this bond with Christ is sealed. Yet this ritual is a symbol for something true for the entire world. We believe Christ saved all of creation. Through baptism we choose to participate consciously in that salvation. Nevertheless, Christ saved the entire world, baptized or not.

That's why we can seek Christ in all persons. We can look for in any person that which is the redeemed image of God. What does this mean? It means to look for that which is risen in one another—that which is beautiful, powerful, and loving. This promise asks us to "seek" out the image of God in others. Not only are we to know that Christ is there within the members of our household; we are actually to go looking for Christ. So when people in our household are being annoying, we try to look for God's image resting on them and Christ's redeeming love dwelling in them. It's easy to love our family members when they are lovable. What this promise asks us to do is choose to love them and remember who they are when they act most unlovable.

Children tend to see the good in others more easily than adults. One day I was madly rushing to prepare the dining room table for a dinner party. In my haste, I knocked over a cruet of olive oil onto the tablecloth. As I watched the oil soak into the cloth, it seemed the last straw in what had been a hectic day. I cried out in frustration. My older daughter, three years old at the time, said, "That's okay, Mommy, you can fix it." I turned and said angrily, "No, it's not okay. It's a disaster. Don't you know that some things just can't be fixed?" Her reaction to my emotional and mean response? She came up to me, gave me a hug, and said, "Don't worry, Mommy. It will be all right. We're a loving family."

My tirade ended immediately. Her words and hug washed the rage and the feelings of inadequacy behind my rage right out of me. She had looked right through my rude behavior and seen the person she loved. She had seen Christ within me and knew that love was there—and responded with love.

I can't always respond so quickly with love when my children throw tantrums or are obstinately disobedient. I'm more likely to respond with exasperation and impatience, illustrating not only how very human I am, but also why this promise is such a necessary component of the Baptismal Covenant. The discipline of seeking Christ in others, of taking the time to discern what is good and loving about them, of acknowledging the gifts they have to offer, can be hard work at times. Yet if we practice this discipline, not only will we respond more lovingly to those around us, but we will also mature in our own faith. Seeking Christ in others reinforces the image of

God within us. It helps us to honor Christ within us. It compels us to live deeper into our own baptized lives.

We also promise to serve Christ in one another. If we choose to be conscious of the love that dwells within the people we see every day (and share the bathroom with), then we can also choose how we act toward these folks. To serve Christ in other people is to honor them, to treat them with graciousness and respect. From a parent's perspective, this promise is also about helping our children discover Christ within themselves and then affording them opportunities to love others.

Listening for What Is Real

One of the ways we serve Christ in one another is to actively look and listen for the truth amid all the distortion. We can listen for the truth within ourselves, which can help us more readily hear the truth coming from our children. Practicing active listening as parents helps us to know our own motivations and to be more ready to see what our children are up to rather than jumping to conclusions. You know how attuned your ears are to your child's cry. Not only can you distinguish your infant's cry from another's; you can also determine what kind of cry you hear on the playground. Without looking up, I could tell whether my daughters were crying out in pain, exuberance, or frustration. This attuned listening can be applied to the rest of life. When our kids speak out in anger, we can listen for what is behind that anger. Is fear or confusion the real issue? When our children don't follow directions, it's helpful to understand why. Are they being disobedient, or did they honestly not understand what we asked? As parents, we need to listen for what is real.

On more than one occasion, when I've said no to my daughters and stuck with it, their response was less than charming. "Why can't I watch another show? You're torturing me! If you don't let me watch more TV, I'm not going to speak to you ever, ever again!" At first glance these expressions seem to constitute extremely disrespectful, out-of-bounds behavior that must be stopped at all costs. But that would be a distortion. Active listening tells me that my daughter is simply angry and disappointed that she can't watch any more TV, but she's overwhelmed and tired at the moment and doesn't have control of her emotions. After all, how many times do we as adults lose our self-control? By acting calmly and reiterating my point, I respond to the situation rather than to the emotion: "Nevertheless, you've already had your TV time for today, and it's time to turn it off." My daughter storms out of the room shouting, "I hate you!" accompanied by a door slam. I let her go. Minutes later, she returns, having come to herself. She knows the rules. In her heart she knows I'm not being unreasonable but just applying the normal household limit on TV. "I'm sorry I yelled at you, Mommy," she apologizes. Had I responded to her angry outburst with one of my own (which I've done on more than one occasion!), the emotions would have run high and the situation become more entangled. But by giving her a chance to calm down and by not taking her angry words at face value, I can initiate a calm conversation about her behavior: "When you yell at me like that, I feel disrespected because those are harsh words. I want you to speak respectfully." Thus, I'm able to model for her a response that helps her see and modify her behavior but doesn't put her down as a person.

The above example illustrates a parenting technique called the use of "I" statements. I learned this technique from a parenting classes taught by Julie Ross of Parenting Horizons in New York.[16] Many parenting books and techniques are helpful in guiding us to parent with wisdom and love. Parenting is a difficult job and one that changes as our children grow and change. There's no reason to assume we should naturally know what to do. We need our own examples to follow. It's also helpful to have friends who are parents and who share some of your values. Sometimes we get caught in unhelpful patterns of behavior but don't see them clearly. Having friends with whom you can share your struggles and who will tell you honestly if they think you're going astray is an invaluable parenting aid.

The use of "I" statements is a two-way street. Sometimes the behavior roles are reversed. Sometimes I'm the one with the angry outburst and my daughters articulate how my behavior makes them feel. It's quite humbling to hear a six-year-old say, "Mommy, when you use your loud voice, I feel scared and it hurts my feelings." It's humbling—and encouraging—because it demonstrates that my children are learning how to recognize and communicate their feelings. They know I love them and are able to name the distortion caused by my anger. This gives me the opportunity to repent, to apologize, and to come to myself. And that is a great gift.

Serving Christ

Serving Christ in our children isn't the same as giving in to their demands or letting them call all the shots. Yet sometimes out of a sense of loving them, this is what we do. When one of my daughters was three, she seemed to demand a snack at every bedtime. Not wanting to send her to bed hungry, I gave in. But it upset the entire bedtime routine, and I knew that eating right before bedtime isn't the best thing for a good night's sleep. But I seemed caught. When I shared my dilemma with a friend, she said outright—and lovingly—"That girl is playing you. She is not going to starve before breakfast." Her words helped me see how my child's demands were really about delaying bedtime; as a result, I was able to adjust my parenting. I simply asked my daughter earlier in the evening if she was hungry, gave her a chance to have a final snack an hour before bedtime, and told her there'd be no more food until breakfast. I stuck with it—and it worked. She stopped asking to eat at bedtime, and calm returned to our evening routine.

Serving Christ in your own child can be daunting and humbling. It means allowing yourself to be affected by your child, being vulnerable with your child, admitting that your child may have things to teach you. It doesn't mean becoming your child's waiter. I watched a father at a softball game allow his son to call all the shots. It was time to collect equipment after a game. "Where's your glove?" the father asked. "Over there somewhere," the eight-year-old replied, pointing. "Can't you keep all your stuff together?" the father asked in exasperation, then proceeded to walk to where his son had pointed to pick up the glove. Meanwhile, his son continued to talk to his friends. It seemed that father and son had played this scenario many times before. Rather than serving Christ in his son, the father was in fact doing the opposite. By picking up the glove himself, he was discouraging his son from being responsible for his own equipment. At the same time, the father was encouraging his son to ignore the presence of Christ in his father. The son was treating his father with disrespect and wasn't being called on it.

I'm sure the father didn't set out to let his son rule that day. Sometimes we don't always notice our actions. But allowing your kids to behave disrespectfully is not serving Christ in them. It's giving away your authority as the parent. Serving Christ in others means treating them respectfully and asking for and expecting the same respect in return. We'll take a close look at the importance of respect in the next chapter. Really honoring that child would have involved calling that child to honor himself. The exchange might have gone like this:

> *"Son, time to go—please gather up your equipment."*
> *"I don't know where my glove is."*
> *"Where did you put it?"*
> *"It's over there somewhere."*
> *"Then you need to stop talking to your friends and go get it."*
> *"Can't you get it for me?"*
> *"When you don't keep track of your equipment yourself, I feel concerned that you might lose your glove. I want you to go find it yourself."*
> *"Okay. I'll see you later, guys—I have to go get my glove."*

In this case, the father is clear about his expectations. He speaks respectfully to his son. When at first his son doesn't follow directions, the father explains his concern and reiterates his request. The son can hear the reasonableness of the expectation and respond respectfully to his father. He has the opportunity to practice responsibility, which in turn will help him become a mature, responsible adult. It's simply not loving to raise a child to expect that things will always be done for him.

Serving Christ in others is giving them what they need. If they are hungry, give them something to eat. If they are thirsty, give them something to drink. If they are lonely, give them companionship. If they don't know what to do with their lives, give them an arena in which to discover and live out their gifts. Serving Christ in others includes giving them the support they need to live out their own potential. When it comes to parenting our children, we need to help them see, honor, and develop their gifts. We need to help them become aware of their capabilities and learn to listen to the world around them so they can recognize and respond to the hunger, thirst, and loneliness they encounter. We need to give them the tools to seek and serve Christ in others.

Not Giving Advice

When I sought out my friend's help with the bedtime snack issue, I was looking for guidance. Her perception was helpful. She listened lovingly and responded from her heart. She didn't tell me what to do. Giving advice is not the same as serving others. In fact, giving advice often stops us from practicing active listening. When we are in advice mode, rather than listening to a person, we listen for a problem that can be solved. When we focus on fixing something, we can fail to really understand what is going on. One time with a group of adults, I told a personal story about a poignant parenting dilemma. One member of the group immediately began to give me advice about how to handle the situation. But I wasn't looking for advice. I wanted to share the pain I had felt about a parenting moment I knew had gone badly. I'd chosen to be vulnerable about my limitations. As this person began to tell me what I could have done, I realized she hadn't heard the real pain I wanted to share. She missed the significance of what was really redemptive for me, which was telling the story.

It's especially easy to fall into the trap of "fixing" when as parents we mediate problems. I think it helps to develop a discipline of listening, of discerning what is really being said by the words and actions of our children. For me, this sometimes means literally sitting on my hands and working to keep my mouth shut. Children need the opportunity to work through their struggles with our support—but without our interference—so that they will have the skills to solve their difficulties when we are not present. If we "take over" every conflict, not only might we be solving the wrong problem (because we didn't take the time to discern what was really at issue), but we may do our children the disservice of not allowing them to try their own hand at solving it. Loving parenting is often about striking a balance between overhelping our children and abandoning them all together. It is this balance we have to seek again and again as both we and our children learn from one another.

Setting Limits

One of the most loving ways to parent is to set limits for our children and stick to them. When it comes to parenting, discipline is often confused with punishment. Exercising discipline is about helping our children learn to make good choices. Punishment is often about taking out our anger on children when they misbehave. As parenting educator Julie Ross writes:

Discipline is a key component of high self-esteem. The two are not mutually exclusive, rather they are inseparable. Discipline refers to how parents set limits for their children. These limits help children define who they are. Only after discovering who they are can they then feel good about that person. Adhering to parental limits helps children feel confident and capable about themselves, and promotes an "I can do it" feeling.[17]

Some friends of mine had excellent results setting limits as parents. They had established allowances for their children at about age four. They set a tone from the start that assumed that any toys their children wanted apart from birthday or Christmas gifts were things the children needed to save their own money for. One Christmas their son received a couple of books from a series. He wanted more, sooner rather than later, and not from the library, but to own. Rather than buying them for him, his parents helped him figure out how to save his money. Over the ensuing months, he purchased quite a few of those books himself. He was very happy to own them, and his parents were happy to see him reading and rereading them. They felt good about their limit setting.

Then one week he came home from school with an order form from a book club and showed his parents a $20 computer game that he wanted in the worst way. His mother said, "Well, you don't have $20 right now."

He checked his piggy bank; he only had about $6.

His mother suggested that she could buy it and put it away until he had accumulated the money to pay for it. He readily agreed to the plan.

Had this couple not set limits with earlier and smaller purchases, they easily could have subjected themselves to much cajoling, whining, and harassing about the computer game. In truth, this is their experience of what happens when situations arise for which they haven't set limits. They've learned that it is worth being consistent and firm on these matters. Otherwise, they must be prepared to deal with the inevitable whining or to give in and feel very uncomfortable about it.

It's also admirable to note the expectations they established along with their use of an allowance. Whatever the amount of their weekly allowance, each of their children is required to set aside 10 percent for the church offering and 20 percent for their long-term savings. What is left over is for themselves and can be used for immediate gratification or their own savings plans. Not only have these children learned the value of respecting the limits they encounter; they are also learning the value of setting limits for themselves.

Paying Attention

Another way to show love to others is to give them our serious attention. I once watched in admiration as a speaker gave his complete attention to someone who asked him a question. I was attending a large conference at which this well-known writer gave a keynote address. The room of almost five hundred attendees was mesmerized. During the break that followed, a line formed of people who wanted to ask him a question. I was in that line. I watched as this quiet man gave his rapt attention to a woman as she asked her question. He focused completely on her, not concerned about the line of people behind her, the shortness of the break, or the commotion that surrounded them as the room was prepared for the next conference activity. I thought at the time how much he honored her. We do honor others when we give them our complete attention. We let them know that who they are and what they have to say are important. Giving this kind of attention is one of the ways we can communicate God's love. It's also a way in which we can receive God's love. When we give someone our full attention, we are also opening ourselves up to the surprising gifts they have to share with us; we are acknowledging that they have something of value to give us. In fact, God's love is often revealed to us in unexpected encounters with others. As Paul Donoghue writes in *The Jesus Advantage*, "We need to pay attention to God communicating to us through all of his creation, but especially through those whom he has given us to love."[18] When we pay attention to those in our household, to our children, and really listen to them, we not only practice love, but also open ourselves to holy encounters.

Loving Our Neighbor

It all comes down to treating your children as you want to be treated. This is the "love your neighbor as yourself" part. There is perhaps no better place to practice love of neighbor than in our very own homes. As Thomas Breidenthal writes in *Christian Households*, "Is there any difference between encountering the neighbor in the utter stranger and being brought up short by the unexpected otherness of one's spouse or child?"[19]

Our homes can model in a small way what God's entire kingdom might look like. It is in our homes, with those who live there, that we get to practice loving our neighbor. It's here that we live out our Baptismal Covenant daily. Young children, in particular, are first formed by their home life, nurtured by their primary caregivers. It is in this place that they will first learn about what a community is and can be. As they grow older, they become more involved with other institutions, such as schools, churches, and sports and activity centers. If their primary household is one in which they are valued and are expected to value others, then they will carry this attitude and the behaviors it engenders to all other communities they encounter.

Choosing to Love

Often, loving parenting is about choosing to take loving action when that is not what we feel like doing. We can choose to make loving decisions in our households.

The chaotic morning rush to get everyone off to work and school used to just about kill me. One of the funniest moments came one morning when I was trying to get out the door but at the last minute couldn't find my keys. In a fit of exasperation, I dropped all my bags, threw my coat on the floor, and kicked off my shoes, which went flying. When I had calmed down a bit later, one of my shoes was nowhere to be found. We all looked for it. We knew it had to be somewhere in the front hallway. We finally found it hanging on the coat tree. We all laughed. I was somewhat chagrined to think of the story my first grader might tell her teacher that day, of her wild mother who kicked her shoe into the coat tree in a fit of annoyance. But that's what happened.

I resolved to do better. And this is what I discovered: we all had different needs in the morning, but we all shared the need to get ready for the day. While my children were quite independent and capable of managing most of their morning routine, I couldn't expect them to get themselves completely ready while my husband and I were getting dressed at the same time. We needed to plan the morning better. I began to get up a bit earlier and do all my own preparations first. Then there was time to focus on the kids and do one thing at a time rather than five or ten. It's true that parenting teaches you very quickly to multitask; nevertheless, there are only ten minutes between 8:20 and 8:30 no matter how you manage it. You can only do ten minutes' worth of tasks. Changing our morning game plan to include reasonable expectations for everyone made all the difference in the world.

Our daughters prepare differently in the morning. One can be depended upon to get dressed quickly with only one prompt, but needs more parenting at the breakfast table. The other one can prepare her own breakfast, but without some coaching may well be reading a book instead of getting dressed. As the parent, I needed to honor their needs and differences and adjust. I had to adjust not only to get my own needs met, but also to parent my children and help them get their needs met. Of course, my husband and I also prepare differently in the morning, so it's just as anxiety producing for one of us to have unreasonable expectations of the other parent as it is to have unreasonable expectations of our children. No one's morning needs are more important than another's. On a given day, one person's needs may trump another's (a sick child needs more attention, and what is urgent and important must be dealt with), but all people in the household have reasonable needs.

Household Rituals

One way to love and honor one another in the household is through intentional family rituals. A ritual is a coordinated and repeated event that holds meaning for the participants. A ritual is different than a routine. The way you take your shower and brush your teeth and get dressed every morning is a routine. It is a repeated event but one that doesn't hold much, if any, significant meaning for you. Rituals, on the other hand, carry a great deal of significance and when done well have many positive outcomes. In his book *The Intentional Family: Simple Rituals to Strengthen Family Ties*, psychologist William J. Doherty explores how family rituals bring stability to a household and foster connection among household members. Whether it's a bedtime practice, a birthday celebration, Christmas dinner, or a monthly family hiking outing, these events can be intentionally ritualized.

Creating a family ritual takes time and intentionality. A mealtime can be catch as catch can, or it can become a ritual in which the dinner table is set, everyone sits down at the same time, a candle is lit, grace is said, and all enjoy the meal together. While rituals must be set and dependable in order to be rituals, it's also important to be flexible. The bedtime ritual that works for your two-year-old will need to change as your child grows or as another sibling begins to take part. Rituals that are too rigid may become negative. But rituals that allow us to bond, enjoy one another's company, be intentional about our time together, and show our care for others in the household are great vehicles for seeking and serving Christ in one another and showing our love for the members of our household.

Getting Your Feet Wet

Things to Think About

- When have you recognized Christ in another? How might another recognize Christ in you?
- When is it most difficult for you to see Christ in your child? When is it easiest?
- How do you demonstrate your love to your child? To other members of your household? To yourself?
- In what areas do you need practice loving those in your household as your neighbors?
- When has your child communicated God's love to you?

Things to Do

- Write love letters to your child and place them under their door or in their lunch box.
- Write a prayer praising God for the gift of your child and thanking God for allowing you to be a parent.
- Think about one thing you can do to give yourself more emotional "space" to be an active listener and an attentive presence.

CHAPTER ELEVEN

Peace and Quiet, or Peace and Justice?

"Will you strive for justice and peace among all people and respect the dignity of every human being?"

"Mom! She's not letting me have my turn on the computer!"

I have to admit that my first response to such an outcry is to flee. I absolutely hate mediating disputes. Or more to the point, I absolutely hate disputes altogether. It's unreasonable to expect the members of my household to get along all the time and peace to reign, but I often find myself seduced into just such an expectation. Despite everything I know about human limitations, child development, and community life, I find in myself the desire for my household to simply run smoothly. And that simply doesn't happen. Peaceful households don't just happen. To the extent to which they exist at all, they are the result of intentional hard work and God's grace. They begin with the concept of fairness. There is no peace without justice.

What does justice look like in the home? It's not simply a matter of being fair, although that's a good place to start. One day my girls had over a friend who is an only child. They wanted to watch a video together, so they set out to choose what they wanted to watch. Moments later, the young friend came to me to ask if she could watch a certain video. "You all need to decide together," I told her. She returned to the family room but was back a moment later with a different video in her hand. "Can I watch this one?" she asked. I followed her back into the room, saying, "The three of you need to agree on what to watch." My two daughters were in the midst of negotiations. One would suggest a video, and the other would say, "I don't want to watch that one. How about this one?" Their friend was mystified. It suddenly occurred to me that as an only child, she didn't have a sibling to negotiate with. The only person whose approval and agreement she needed was one of her parents—so she kept coming to me with her request.

In that moment I became aware of having taught my daughters the art of negotiating without even realizing it. This had begun because I refused to keep track of turns. Early on, when my daughters couldn't agree on what to watch, I decided that it would be much too complicated for me to keep track of whose turn it was to make the choice. I wasn't willing to live with a system that dictated that one girl could choose which video to watch one day and the other girl could have her choice the next day. Instead, I told them they had to agree on a choice. I wanted the decision to be in their hands. Soon they learned to say, "I'm not interested in watching that. How about this one?" The more they practiced this negotiation, the better they became at coming to a joint decision quickly. Of course, being thrown into this dynamic without any practice was confusing for their friend. That situation required some work on including others and being hospitable to guests. Nevertheless, their negotiating skills come in handy in many situations.

This isn't an example of brilliant parenting, but rather one of graceful stumbling. I hadn't sat down and thought, "Hmm, negotiating is a good skill to have, so I'd better teach it to my girls." Instead, my solution came as a result of my desire to solve conflict and seek peaceful decisions that didn't require me to referee. If I were a less spiritual person, I would say that the success of my plan was pure luck. But I really think that some of the values that I hold dear came to the fore with the grace of the Holy Spirit. Because I've been taught that it's important to strive for peace and justice, I want not only to enact those values in my household, but also to teach my children to do the same.

While negotiation and consensus building are important skills that promote justice in the household, the concept of taking turns is also important. When it comes to setting the table or deciding which grace to say, it's more helpful in our household to take turns than to engage in elaborate negotiations. Taking turns underscores the value that each family member can contribute to family tasks. Negotiation, consensus building, and taking turns are all tools that help promote justice in the home. As with any task, the right tool always makes the job easier. Choose what makes sense for your household and the situations that arise.

Justice and Equality

By virtue of our baptisms, we are all complete members of the body of Christ. Our children are no less members of that body than we ourselves. And they are not lesser members of the household. The practice of justice in the home is closely linked to an understanding of equality. Each household member, regardless of age or ability, has an equal claim on the privileges that come with membership. This doesn't mean that we set aside our proper authority as parents in order to cater to our children—we have a responsibility to be the adults; to exercise discipline, supply basic needs, provide safety and security, and love and nurture our children. What it does mean is that we keep in mind that our children have an equal claim with us to receive basic needs, safety, security, nurture, and love.

If we are to live out this truth in the home, we need to respect all members of the household and treat all members justly. Striving for peace in a household doesn't mean that things will be quiet and controlled according to the parents' wishes. I remember Julie Ross telling a group of parents that following her suggestions for dealing with sibling rivalry would not guarantee a quieter household. More peaceful, yes, but not quieter. Our desire for peace and quiet as parents may not be the same as a desire for peace and justice. Justice is about understanding the needs and wants of each member as well as the values of the household. I remember the grace that my father often prayed at our dinner table, which included the phrase, "Help us be mindful of the needs and wants of others." Imposing my will on others is not about peace and justice.

In *The Intentional Family*, William Doherty discusses the inherent contradiction of a family model in which the goal is both the stability of the family unit and the achievement of happiness for each individual member. This structure soon unravels. How can stability be maintained when one spouse's need for personal happiness conflicts with that of the other spouse? What happens to the household when each family member expects to have personal needs met and achieve happiness regardless of the others? Rather than moving toward lasting harmony, this family structure often deconstructs, ending in dissatisfaction if not a breakup.

A more helpful model that brings stability and connection is one in which members enjoy one another and work together creatively to build family identity. Doherty calls this the Intentional Family. When members of a household work together, they don't allow one member of the household to make choices at the expense of others. Children's activities are not supported at the expense of the adults' need for personal time. By the same token, adult activities, whether work or pleasure, are not supported at the expense of the children's need for nurture. There must be a just distribution of labor and recreation.

Both of our daughters enjoy taking classes at a local youth theater. When the opportunity arises to audition for plays, we have a family discussion and decision. My husband's work is also in theatre, and when directing a play, he has rehearsals in the evenings and on weekends. When the girls are in plays, they also have rehearsals in the evenings and on weekends. How do we honor the desire of the girls to do something they enjoy, as well as my husband's work schedule, my work schedule, and our limited time and energy? The first time this situation arose, my husband and I decided that as a rule, only one member of our household can be in rehearsal at a time. Doing otherwise causes too much stress. So, when an opportunity for the girls to be in a play arises, we first look at our entire family schedule before agreeing to allow them to audition. While my husband and I as the adults decided on the basic one-play-at-a-time rule, we explained our decision to our daughters. Thus, when we have a family discussion about which plays they can do, the girls know the basic parameters. The same process applies to any activity. Whether it's a sports team the girls want to sign up for, a retreat that I want to lead, or a committee my husband wants to join, we first balance the desire of the one with the needs of the whole. Nor do we assume that the adults get first choice when it comes to extracurricular activities. We try to ensure that each household member can participate in decision making.

Sharing in Tasks, Joys, and Difficult Decisions

A just and peaceful household is one in which all members contribute, as they are able, to managing the household. It is in the household that a child first learns what equality looks like, and it's important that the family model a fair distribution of labor. As children age and their abilities increase, they can share in more household tasks. For the work to be equitable, it's important that no one is expected to participate beyond their ability, including adults. In our house we try to work together. My husband and I divvy up all of the household tasks, from maintaining the lawn to doing laundry to changing the cat litter. When either of us has our responsibilities change at work, we shift the household tasks around to make it work. When it comes to mealtime, we all pitch in. My husband and I take turns with meal preparation: one of us cooks, and the other does the dishes. The girls assist with the cooking, set the table, and clear the dishes.

We also share family joys. We congratulate one another on achievements, great and small. When my husband was given tenure at his college, the girls threw a party for him. They were five and seven at the time and didn't really know what tenure was—but they knew it was important. Their father told them how excited he was and how proud he felt. And we indulged in one of our favorite family celebrations: root beer floats and dancing!

In our weekly family meeting (discussed in chapter 7), we include all household members in decision making. During this time we've discussed everything from birthday party plans to whether we should add a new animal to our household to the girls' desire to tithe to our church. We encourage our girls to bring their own ideas and topics to family meeting time. We are careful not to ask our daughters for their opinions if we don't plan to hear them. There are times when my husband and I make the decisions because we are adults and we have the wisdom to do so, and there are times when we allow the girls to have a choice. Power isn't only about how the children are treated, but also about how the adults interact. Some items on the family meeting agenda, such as scheduling, may be boring for our kids, but at least they get to see how we make decisions. We model for them the give-and-take in being partners who have made a covenant with one another.

We don't use our family meeting time for discipline—that happens separately. But we've included our daughters in decisions about discipline. Once when our older daughter broke the TV rule and lied about it, we asked her what she thought would be a fair consequence. In a contrite voice, she suggested no TV for two weeks. We agreed that her choice of consequence was logical, but we shortened the length of the consequence to what seemed fitting to us. It was a fair and just decision that we made together.

Encouraging equality and justice in the household also means including all members in dinner table conversations, holiday planning, and prayer rituals. Everyone has something to contribute.

Humor

Never underestimate the power of humor to lessen the toxicity of a situation when emotions run high. A friend was making a six-hour car trip with her children, ages three, five, and eight, all sitting side by side in the backseat. About three hours into the ride, they hit big-city traffic with numerous roundabouts and complicated interstate highways; everybody's nerves were frayed. Suddenly the oldest howled with indignation from the backseat: "She just bit me!" My friend snapped back at her youngest, "That's terrible. As soon as I can stop the car, I'm going to bite you!" Total silence followed— then a giggle, then more. Her son said, "Mommy, now she's biting her own arm getting ready for you." The mother replied with a stifled laugh herself and more admonishment about never doing that again to yourself or anyone else. Then they all gave in to hysterical laughter and pulled off at the next rest stop for milkshakes all around.

My friend admits that the story doesn't portray her as a wise, judicious parent, but it did have a good outcome. I think, however, that choosing to stop for milkshakes *was* quite wise and judicious, and so was her ability to laugh at herself and the situation. And while she may not have been happy about how she first responded to the situation, she did turn it into a teachable moment. She took the opportunity to teach her children not to bite and to treat others and themselves gently. And by using humor to turn the situation around, she showed them that hurting someone just because you have been hurt is not justice and does not bring peace to a situation. There were indeed many good outcomes to the situation. And it's a powerful story that she still tells with humor now that her children are grown.

Sometimes we just need to relax about the ridiculous situations we get ourselves into as parents. Peace in a household can be the result of being able to laugh at ourselves, share our good humor at one another's foibles, and celebrate with milkshakes.

Respect for Others

Respect means to "re-spect," to look again. If we wish to honor and respect a piece of artwork that someone has created, we could go about it in this way: Look at it, then look at it again. What do you see? The focus of this way of engaging with someone's work is not about interpretation, but about sensing. Not "What do you think?" or "How does it make you feel?" but "What do you see? What do you hear?" In a like manner we can respect our children and other members of our household. When we're about to respond to them with our feelings and thoughts, we can first stop and look again. How much more could we honor them as human beings beloved of God if we would stop to look and listen before we responded?

Even as loving parents, we can unintentionally brush off our children as unimportant in so many ways. We assume that the thing they want to tell us or show us is unimportant, so we say, "Not now, honey," or "I'm busy," or just "Hmm?" How many times have we as parents not understood the vocabulary of our three-year-old and responded with a "That's nice," not even knowing what the child has said?

Now it's true that there are times when we are busy and cannot leave the pan on the stove to go see what a child wants to show us. Part of teaching a child respect is teaching them to respect you as well. But we are more intentional about our parenting when we begin with the premise that our child has many things to tell, show, and teach us that are worthy of our attention. And to respect this, we need only to look twice before responding.

Not Judge and Jury

To respect also means to look again without applying a value judgment. An important parenting skill is being able to listen to what our children have to offer us without saying, "This is good," or "This is bad," or "I like this," or even "What an interesting idea." Each of those statements carries a judgment with it based on a value about what is good and what is bad. When a child is throwing a fit, our first parenting response might be to tell them to calm down, using a tone of voice that clearly indicates that we disapprove of their behavior. Yet since a tantrum is often the outward sign of a child's inward emotional turmoil, simply telling them to calm down not only communicates to them that their emotion is "bad," but also overlooks what is upsetting them in the first place.

A second parenting attempt might be to ask them, "Why are you so angry?" Yet this response also applies a judgment. Now we have named the emotion for them, and our question still implies that being angry is not a good thing. A more respectful response, one that helps us take a second look at our child, would be to say simply, "You seem angry." That statement simply names an emotion without applying a good or bad tag to it and allows the child to tell us whether or not we have seen the situation well. He might say, "Yes! I am very mad!" Or he might say, "No, I'm disappointed." Or he might say (or even wail), "I don't know what I feel!" His response gives you more information and allows you to adjust your approach. Whether we are children or adults, we are more able to calm down in any situation when we are truly heard.

There are times when it's exactly our job as adults to know our values and to express them clearly to our children. For example, we can't assume that our children will just pick up good manners on their own. If we want them to say please and thank you and not hit people, we need to teach them these things. If we want them to treat others with respect, we have to show them how. Here are some helpful—and respectful—responses:

"Olivia, when you speak to me in that tone of voice, I feel disrespected because I think you are being rude. I want you to speak respectfully."

"Ariana, when you continue to tackle your brother after he has asked you to stop, I feel angry because I think you are hurting him. I want you to stop now."

"Isaiah, I know that Josh's parents allow him to watch grown-up movies, but we make different choices in our family."

"Please" Is Not a Magic Word

One of the most basic ways we can respect the people in our households is to practice common courtesy. In writing to an early Christian community, the apostle Paul instructs, "As God's chosen ones, holy and beloved, clothe yourselves with compassion, kindness, humility, meekness, and patience" (Colossians 3:12). It can be so easy to forget to use our good manners in the household. If we expect our children to say please and thank you when they are in public, then we need to say please and thank you to one another in our homes. Good manners matter. When we say please and thank you to one another on a daily basis, we're honoring each other. Thus, "please" and "thank you" become deeply theological words. They say, "I honor you; you are worthy of my respect; I see the image of God in you, and I will honor you." We never taught our girls that "please" is the magic word, but we did teach them to use it. When one of them would demand something, we would simply prompt her to change her language and thus her attitude.

> "I want a glass of water!"
> "How could you get that?"
> "May I please have a glass of water?"

This gentle prompt teaches children the difference between a demand and a request. It insists that they treat those around them with respect. It reminds them that common courtesy is expected in the household. Soon they embody the practice of speaking respectfully and don't need to be prompted.

Teaching children that "please" is a magic word undermines the power of manners. It tells them that getting what they want is a matter of using a password rather than respecting the individuals who can help them. It places the power in the word rather than in the relationships between people. And it belittles the deep respect that can be expressed in the word "please."

Dignity and Desire

Parenting often sets our desires against the needs of our children. A sick child needs our care and requires us to rearrange our well-laid plans for the day; money for a baseball uniform requires us to delay getting a new shirt for ourselves; an infant demands our care in the middle of the night when we'd rather sleep. I can remember as a new mother thinking I'd never ever lie down again with the assurance I could sleep until I woke without being interrupted. Caring for children often means setting aside our own desires, at least temporarily. It can mean not watching a favorite TV show when young children are in the room, forgoing a new car for bicycles and music lessons, or sitting up all night with a sick child when we know we need our rest for an important meeting the next day.

Sometimes these choices are unclear and difficult to make. I'm much more willing to stay home with a sick child when my work schedule is easy to rearrange. When my upcoming workday is full of important demands, I find it stressful to reconcile my desire to care for my child with my desire to do my work well. There is nothing wrong with the desire per se. Wanting to do our work well, to enjoy adult recreation, and to get a good night's sleep is fine. But satisfying our own desires at the expense of the child in our care is not faithful parenting.

It's equally problematic to gratify all of our children's desires at the expense of our own well-being. Driving them to every activity they want to do and forgoing our need for downtime doesn't respect our dignity. It's not just the good of the child or the good of the parent that drives ethical decision making, but the good of the community of the household. The question becomes whether or not a choice we make is based on love. Is it more loving to expose my child to the adult violence of an adventure movie because that's what I want to watch, or to deny my desire in order to protect my child from harmful images that she is too young to process? Is it more loving to enable my child to attend two birthday parties in one afternoon even though I have to give up my workout time at the gym to do so, or to help my child make a choice about which party to attend so that she respects my need for exercise?

Making the loving choice is not always easy or convenient. But I believe when we orient ourselves toward what is loving for the community of the household, we are laying the groundwork that creates an environment in which most members can experience peace and love and happiness and comfort. We are turning toward the love of God rather than separating ourselves from it. When entered into wholeheartedly, parenting can lead us into the grace gained through succumbing to the desire of the other. It can be a growing edge for us, especially if we are ready to receive what our children have to offer—if we are prepared to be vessels for the grace they can teach us.

In this final baptismal promise, we promise to respect the dignity of every human being. This means that we must look twice at people rather than avert our eyes. In our families, it means we must look twice at each other rather than assuming we know who our children, spouses, and partners are. It can be deadly to assume that we don't need to rethink our everyday relationships. It is my personal experience that after twenty years of marriage, there remains mystery in my relationship with my husband. I believe I know him better than any other person on earth. And in so many ways, I don't know him at all. He still deserves my respect. To love him, I must look at him and not assume I know what he is thinking or feeling or wanting or needing.

Getting Your Feet Wet

Things to Think About

- What does dignity mean to you?
- What difficult choice have you had to make recently in which your needs and desires conflicted with those of a member of your household? What process did you go through in making that choice?
- Describe what a "peaceful" home means to you. What might a "just" home look like for your family?
- What is an example, from the life of your family, of humor diffusing a tense situation?

Things to Do

- Try praying this grace at mealtimes:

    Bless our food, dear God, we pray,

    And bless us, too, throughout this day.

    Keep us safe and close to you,

    Keep us just in all we do. Amen.

- Create a designated quiet place or "peace room" in your home where no fighting is allowed and to which anyone can retreat for some guaranteed downtime.

- Model respectful speaking to your child. Prompt them when necessary:
  "Give me my book!"
  "How would you get that?"
  "Would you please give me my book?"
  "Certainly, and thank you for asking so nicely," or "Certainly, as soon as I finish carrying these dishes to the kitchen."

CHAPTER TWELVE

Loving Yourself

For each of us, our life's work is to be the person God created us to be. Parenting is a vocation, a calling. When entered into wholeheartedly, parenting encourages us daily to discover and use our gifts to become better people. Choosing to baptize our children is a loving choice that allows us to place our parenting in the context of faith. To choose parenting and to choose baptism are both acts of faith; they both take the plunge into unknown waters. But these waters are not uncharted. Many have entered them before and know their depths. The baptismal rite underscores this truth. We make our promises "with God's help." We are surrounded by family, friends, and our faith community.

Part of the Baptismal Covenant—and perhaps the most basic tenet of the Christian faith—is Jesus' command that we love our neighbors as ourselves. Neighbors are strangers with whom we share borders. Regardless of how well we know the members of our households, we'll never know them as thoroughly as God does, and in many respects they'll always be strangers to us. We must be ready for the possibility of border skirmishes within our families. Members may not love the same things. Siblings may not be friends. We need to make space for these realities. This doesn't mean we give up loving. On the contrary, we must practice loving all the more faithfully. Despite the fairy tales many of us grew up with, people just don't simply live "happily ever after." Rather, parenting and creating a household are an adventure.

In the movie *Spy Kids*, retired international spy Ingrid Cortez tells her daughter a bedtime story about two spies who fell in love and embarked on "the most dangerous mission of all time": marriage and family. She explains to her daughter that when the spies retired and became parents, "they exchanged one life of adventure for another, trading espionage for parenthood: a mysterious and compelling mission in its own right."[20] My husband

and I are still in the early stages of this parenting adventure, and already it has brought us more than we could possibly imagine. It's an adventure I am glad not to have missed.

Like parenting, loving your neighbor as yourself is a two-way street. You have to care for yourself if you are going to love your children. When our first daughter was born, we had the best pediatrician in the world. Before we took our daughter home from the hospital, he gave us two assignments: before she was a week old, we had to take her out in public; and before she was a month old, we had to go out on a date without her. He was serious and asked us if we had fulfilled these assignments on our follow-up visits. He was a wise man. The first assignment helped us not to be paralyzed by the fear of parenting, the anxiety that our newborn was so fragile and precious that we might break her. It kept us from confining her and ourselves to our home, unable to face the world. The second assignment was about caring for ourselves, about remembering who we were as partners and lovers. It demanded that we trust others to care for our daughter, that we learn from the get-go that parenting is a community effort.

What is it to gain the whole world only to lose our souls? asks Jesus. What is it to save the whole world only to lose our families? I wonder. So many things begin at home. It is where we learn to love and be loved, or to hurt and be hurt—or some of both. As parents, we have a very important job to do: raising our children. Teaching them. Loving them. Thus, the home is the first place we must begin to live out this covenant if we are truly going to live it out in the world. Not only because it's practice, but also because it will feed us. I have found it true over and over again that when I'm overwhelmed at work—whether by emotionally charged events, the sheer amount of stuff to do, or plain stress—if I focus on my relationships at home, it always makes a difference. If I ground myself in the love of my husband and children, I'm better equipped to face the world with grace and a sense of God's presence.

The more I write and teach about baptism, the more I become aware of the depth of the relationship that God offers us. Even writing this book has changed my understanding of baptism and allowed me to dive deeper into the waters of my faith. I have also learned more about myself as a parent and a spouse, and I am grateful to my husband and girls for teaching me so much about who I am, who they are, and who we are as a household. The psalmist prays, "The LORD looks down from heaven upon us all to see if there is any who is wise, if there is one who seeks after God" (Psalm 14:2, BCP). To be wise is to seek after God. It seems to me that it takes much wisdom to parent well. What better way to start than to seek God through baptism. Ultimately, baptism is a loving choice, both for our children and for ourselves as parents.

Getting Your Feet Wet

Things to Think About

- What are you doing for yourself to help you better understand whom God has uniquely created you to be?
- Which of your gifts do you use most in parenting?
- Which of the five Baptismal Covenant promises poses the most difficulties for you? Which one is most comfortable?
- What is one thing that you can do to take better care of yourself? Of your primary relationships? How can you put those things into practice?

Things to Do

- Plan a night out for yourself and your spouse or close friend. Enjoy some rejuvenating adult time.
- Create a photo album, slideshow, or scrapbook that tells the story of your life as a parent.
- Write a prayer thanking God for the gift of parenting and all that it has taught you.

RESOURCES

BAPTISM

Pritchard, Gretchen Wolff. *New Life.* New Haven, CT: The Sunday Paper, 1986.

Wangerin, Walter, Jr. *Water, Come Down! The Day You Were Baptized.* Minneapolis: Augsburg Fortress Publishers, 1999.

RITUAL

Doherty, William. *The Intentional Family: Simple Rituals to Strengthen Family Ties.* New York: HarperCollins, 1997; reprint 2002.

Kitch, Anne E. *The Anglican Family Prayer Book.* Harrisburg, PA: Morehouse Publishing, 2004.

Nelson, Gertrud Mueller. *To Dance with God: Family Ritual and Community Celebration.* New York: Paulist Press, 1986.

Travnikar, Rock, OFM. *The Blessing Cup: 40 Simple Rituals for Family Prayer-Celebrations.* Cincinnati: St. Anthony Messenger Press, 1994.

PRAYER

Denham, Joyce. *A Child's Book of Celtic Prayers.* Oxford: Lion Hudson, 1998.

Farrington, Debra K. *Unceasing Prayer: A Beginner's Guide.* Brewster, MA: Paraclete Press, 2002.

Kelly, Marcia and Jack. *One Hundred Graces.* New York: Bell Tower, 1992.

Roth, Nancy L. *Praying: A Book for Children.* New York: The Church Hymnal Corporation, 1991.

Weber, Christopher L. *Give Us Grace: An Anthology of Anglican Prayers.* Harrisburg, PA: Morehouse Publishing, 2004.

PARENTING

Fuchs-Kreimer, Nancy. *Parenting as a Spiritual Journey: Deepening Ordinary & Extraordinary Events into Sacred Occasions.* Woodstock, VT: Jewish Lights Publishing, 2002.

Haffner, Debra W. *From Diapers to Dating.* New York: Newmarket Press, 2000; reprint 2004.

Ross, Julie A. *Practical Parenting for the 21st Century.* New York: Excalibur Publishing, 1993.

CHILDREN'S BOOKS

Alexander, Cecil Francis. *All Things Bright and Beautiful.* Illustrated by Preston McDaniels. Harrisburg, PA: Morehouse Publishing, 2000.

Brett, Jan. *On Noah's Ark.* New York: Putnam, 2003.

De Paolo, Tomie. *Tomie DePaolo's Book of Bible Stories.* New York: Putman, 1990.

Polacco, Patricia. *Chicken Sunday.* New York: Philomel Books, 1992.

Sasso, Sandy Eisenberg. *In God's Name.* Woodstock, VT: Jewish Lights Publishing, 1994.

Thompson, Lauren. *Love One Another.* New York: Scholastic Press, 2000.

Wildsmith, Brian. *Exodus.* Grand Rapids, MI: Eerdmans, 1999.

Wood, Douglas. *Grandad's Prayers of the Earth.* Cambridge, MA: Candlewick Press, 1999.

———. *Old Turtle.* Duluth, MN: Pfeifer-Hamilton Publishers, 1992.

MUSIC AND VIDEOS

Beall, Pamela Conn, and Susan Hagen Nipp. *Wee Sing Bible Songs.* CD and book edition. Los Angeles: Price Stern Sloan, 2005.

NEST Family Entertainment animated Bible stories. www.nestentertainment.com.

VeggieTales animated Bible stories. www.bigidea.com.

NOTES

1. William J. Doherty, *The Intentional Family: Simple Rituals to Strengthen Family Ties* (New York: HarperCollins, 1997; reprint 2002), 10.

2. The Book of Common Prayer (New York: Oxford University Press, 1979).

3. Orthodox Jewish women still practice a very similar ritual today. Also, prior to the 1979 edition, The Book of Common Prayer contained a service called "The Thanksgiving of Women after Child-birth" that was modeled after the Jewish ritual. It has been replaced by "Thanksgiving for the Birth or Adoption of a Child" in the 1979 edition.

4. For a more thorough discussion of the historical development of the baptismal rite, see Daniel Stevick, *Baptismal Moments, Baptismal Meanings* (New York: The Church Hymnal Corporation, 1987), 5–26.

5. Bill Lewellis (sermon, Grace Church, Allentown, PA, Trinity Sunday, 2004). See also the introduction in William Sloane Coffin, *Credo* (Louisville, KY: Westminster John Knox Press, 2004).

6. Marion J. Hatchett, *Commentary on the American Prayer Book* (New York: Seabury Press, 1981), 274.

7. Thomas E. Breidenthal, *Christian Households: The Sanctification of Nearness* (Cambridge, MA: Cowley, 1997), 22.

8. Sophia Kitch-Peck © 2000.

9. Lucy Kitch-Peck © 2003.

10. Douglas Wood, *Grandad's Prayers of the Earth*, illustrated by P. J. Lynch (Cambridge, MA: Candlewick Press, 1999).

11. Richard I. Cluett (sermon, Cathedral Church of the Nativity, Bethlehem, PA, September 11, 2005).

12. Anne Lamott, *Traveling Mercies: Some Thoughts on Faith* (New York: Pantheon, 1999), 131, 134.

13. Anne E. Kitch, *The Anglican Family Prayer Book* (Harrisburg, PA: Morehouse, 2004), 81–82.

14. Paul J. Donoghue, *The Jesus Advantage: A New Approach to a Fuller Life* (Notre Dame, IN: Ave Maria Press, 2001), 66.

15. Debra W. Haffner, *From Diapers to Dating* (New York: Newmarket Press, 2000; reprint 2004), 6.

16. Newsletters and information about parenting classes can be found at www.parentinghorizons.com. See also Julie A. Ross, *Practical Parenting for the 21st Century* (New York: Excalibur Publishing, 1993).

17. Julie A. Ross, article found at paretninghorizons.com.

18. Donoghue, *Jesus Advantage*, 73.

19. Breidenthal, *Christian Households*, 35.

20. *Spy Kids*, videocassette, directed by Robert Rodriguez (Burbank, CA: Dimension Films; distributed by Buena Vista Home Entertainment, 2001).